A
Life
≫ of ≪
Wholeness

A Life of Wholeness

Reflections on Abundant Living

Revised Edition

Ann Raber, Revision Editor
with John Rogers and Mary Ellen Martin

HERALD PRESS
Scottdale, Pennsylvania
Waterloo, Ontario

Library of Congress Cataloging-in-Publication Data
A Life of wholeness : reflections on abundant living / Ann Raber,
    revision editor, with John Rogers and Mary Ellen Martin. —
        Rev. ed.
        p. cm.
    Includes bibliographical references.
    ISBN 0-8361-3646-2
    1. Conduct of life. 2. Christian life—Mennonite authors.
I. Raber, Ann. II. Rogers, John, 1951- . III. Martin, Mary Ellen.
BJ1581.2.L49 1993
248.4'897—dc20   93-19617
                                                        CIP

The paper used in this publication is recycled and meets the
minimum requirements of American National Standard for
Information Sciences—Permanence of Paper for Printed Library
Materials, ANSI Z39.48-1984.

Unless otherwise noted, Scripture quotations are taken from the
Holy Bible: New International Version. Copyright © 1973, 1978, 1984
International Bible Society. Used by permission of Zondervan
Bible Publishers. All rights reserved.

Scripture quotations marked NEB are from *The New English Bible.* ©
The Delegates of the Oxford University Press and the Syndics of
the Cambridge University Press 1961, 1970. Reprinted with
permission.

Scripture quotations marked NRSV are from the *New Revised
Standard Version Bible*, copyright 1989, by the Division of Christian
Education of the National Council of the Churches of Christ in the
USA, and is used by permission.

A LIFE OF WHOLENESS
Revised edition copyright © 1993 by Herald Press, Scottdale, Pa. 15683
    Published simultaneously in Canada by Herald Press,
    Waterloo, Ont. N2L 6H7. All rights reserved
Library of Congress Catalog Number: 93-19617
International Standard Book Number: 0-8361-3646-2
Printed in the United States of America
Cover and book design by Gwen M. Stamm

1 2 3 4 5 6 7 8 9 10 98 97 96 95 94 93

Contributors

Beryl Brubaker Professor of Nursing, Head of the Nursing Department, Eastern Mennonite College, Harrisonburg, Va.; member of Park View Mennonite Church, Harrisonburg. Appendix

Ronald Hunsicker Director of Pastoral Care and Education, Presbyterian Medical Center of Philadelphia; member of Akron Mennonite Church, Akron, Pa. Chapters three, six, seven and ten.

Willard Krabill Executive Secretary of Mennonite Medical Association; Health Ethics consultant for Mennonite Mutual Aid; member of the College Mennonite Church, Goshen, Ind. Chapters one, three and eight.

Lavonne Platt Owner of Wordsworth where she works as freelance writer, editor and publisher; member of Bethel College Mennonite Church, North Newton, Kan. Chapters four, five, eight and nine.

Bruce Yoder Pastor of Richmond Mennonite Fellowship, Richmond, Va. Chapters two, ten, eleven, and twelve.

Contents

Preface

Mennonite Mutual Aid (MMA—an organization of the Mennonite Church devoted to providing various forms of health and other aid) has a history of concern for health and wellness. It was in 1981, under MMA sponsorship, that this book first began to take shape. Capably guided by editors John Rogers and Mary Ellen Martin, the five writers of the book brought a wealth of knowledge and experience to the project.

In 1990, as part of MMA's continuing commitment to health and wellness, we began to talk about updating this book, and I as an MMA employee assumed responsibility for revisions. Mennonite Publishing House (which had originally released the book under the imprint of its Congregational Literature Division) was also interested and the project became a cooperative one. Eventually it was determined that Herald Press, the book division of Mennonite Publishing House, should release this edition.

Prior to revising this work, I had been pleased to encourage use of this book's previous edition. Many small groups and Sunday school classes found discussion of these chapters stimulating.

More conversation is needed, however. The need to learn more about wellness continues. Until we think as much about living a healthy lifestyle as we do about treatment of disease, there remains a need to continue pondering the "whole" way of life.

As I took on responsibility for reviewing and revising their material, I was happy for the opportunity to work with the great group of five writers whose work forms the heart of this book. It has been a pleasure to note the effective ways in which the contributors, though speaking from a variety of fields, offer the same message—we owe care to our ourselves, each other, our communities, and our earth.

Too many people to be named worked on this revision, but their contributions are not forgotten. One person, however, must be named. Denise Hoffer deserves much credit for all the work she put into word processing. She spent hours on corrections and changes, and her suggestions were always helpful.

Now here is *A Life of Wholeness*, with a message that continues to be fresh and significant. We have the opportunity to move into the next century with an enriched understanding of our own well-being and that of others. From all of us who helped put this resource together to all of you who read it—we wish you much joy as you live "a life of wholeness."

—*Ann Raber*
Goshen, Indiana

Introduction

"I am come that you might have life and have it more abundantly," Jesus said. When we become Christians we are given new life, but we have to do our part to make this life abundant. This study offers practical suggestions for abundant living. Too often our lives are cluttered with worry and stress, our inactivity leaves us with little energy or vitality, and we feel lonely and joyless. This is not the abundant life Jesus had in mind.

We are flooded with information about health and illness. Advertising tells us we need to buy equipment, clothes, and designer foods to be healthy. We are sold expensive programs for exercising, for weight loss, for better nutrition. We are told of the dangers in our cooking utensils, our water, our air, and our homes. Health has become something we pay for rather than create.

But abundant life is not for sale. Living abundantly has to do with what we believe. We can be physically fit as individuals, but we can only be *well* in community. Relationships are an integral part of our reason for living. As people shaped by Anabaptist principles, we understand living in community to be an expression of our Christian faith. Caring for ourselves and each other is a significant part of our stewardship assignment.

Many of us have done a better job of caring for others than for ourselves. And all of us are slow to learn care for our planet. We are discovering how destructive our lack of respect for our bodies and our world really is. We are identifying more linkages between our faith and our health. We can no longer deny that our beliefs, emotions, and relationships affect our personal health and the health of our communities. These are the key themes of this book.

We still have much to learn and to share. If we are to embrace the earth as our present cherished home, if we are to carry out our mission of taking the gospel to all people of the earth, if we are to live abundantly, we need to be making faithful choices that will result in our living a life of wholeness. This book can be a beginning on that rewarding journey. I wish you WELL.

A
Life
≽ of ≼
Wholeness

1

A Life of Wholeness

What Is Wholeness?

Wholeness is being all we can be, developing all the parts of us necessary to be complete—not perfect—persons. Health, wellness, and wholeness are three words for the state of mind, body, and spirit to which we aspire and which the Bible promotes. It is clear from this definition of wholeness that each of us can be whole, despite physical condition or societal evaluation.

A brief glance at the world and those about us reveals how sadly wholeness is missing and how desperately people are struggling to achieve it.

In our fractured, fragmented, impersonal world, Jesus Christ shows us the way to wholeness in his words and his life. Unfortunately, the church has allowed a dualism to creep into its message over the centuries. This dualism separates our bodies from our souls and gives us a low view of the physical body, sometimes causing us to regard ourselves as souls trapped in carnal bodies. Such a negative attitude toward the physical body not only turns many people away from the Christian faith but also results in our taking the stewardship of our bodies less seriously.

The Whole Person

Granger Westberg, Lutheran clergyman, educator, and leader in the wholistic health movement, points out that at one time the spiritual adviser and the physician were the same person. In many primitive societies today the medicine man or witch doctor fulfills this dual function. However, during the Age of Enlightenment and with the rise of science, the body somehow became separated from the emotions and the spirit. Those who studied and treated the body became steadily more isolated from those who ministered to the spiritual life of persons. The rise of the medical profession as we know it today was the result.

A wholistic view, on the other hand, affirms the oneness of the human personality. Each element of the person— body, mind, and spirit—is integrally joined to every other element. What affects one element affects the others also. The elements of personhood are not distinct; rather, they are different aspects of the whole person.

Thus a problem in the body affects one's emotions, and vice versa. We are familiar with the natural tendency to be angry and resentful when physical disability occurs. We are less familiar with the way emotional and spiritual disorders cause our bodies to malfunction.

We have heard the expression "You make me sick!" As Westberg says, this happens to be a folk expression of a real truth. Negative attitudes and interpersonal relationships often do make us sick. Our new understanding of the role of stress in causing physical illnesses and accidents further demonstrates the way in which everything about us is related to everything else.

Our outlook on life does affect our physical health. Attitudes affect bodily functions. For instance, resentment and revenge are associated with the poorest possible functioning of our bodies. Studies are showing that social ills cause physical ills—for example, a sick economy makes people sick. Unemployment is a major stimulus to a rise in the suicide rate. Lonely people have a significantly lower life expectancy. Loneliness, alienation, and isolation do contribute to premature death.

Most important, Westberg shows us both the possibility of and requirements for achieving wholeness. Well-being in all three areas is necessary if we are to experience wholeness. We cannot be whole while neglecting our relationship with God. And we cannot be righteous (spiritually healthy) while neglecting or abusing our physical bodies.

The Bible Affirms Wholeness

In John 5 Jesus did not address only the physical infirmity of the man at the poolside. He sought him out later and told him, "See, you are well again. Stop sinning or something worse may happen to you" (v. 14). When Jesus restored sight to the man in John 9, he also addressed the issue of the relationship of sin, physical health, and faith. In Acts 3:1-10 Peter healed the beggar at the Beautiful Gate, not in some impersonal, mechanistic way, but in a very personal, arresting way.

Called to see persons for who they are—physical-spiritual-social beings—we understand that health is wholeness in all of life. That is the abundant life Jesus came to offer.[1]

The unity of body and spirit is taken for granted in 1 Thessalonians 5:23 and 3 John, verse 2. Mark 12:30 observes that we have heart, soul, mind, and physical body (strength) with which to love God wholly. Romans 12:1-2 regards the presentation of holy bodies to a pleased God as a spiritual service. The integration of physical and spiritual health is further seen in Matthew 9:22, "Your faith has healed you." And Mark 6:56 notes that "all who touched him were healed."

Salvation comes from a word that means "being made whole." A second word important to the concept of wholeness—a word rich in both spiritual and medical meaning—is *shalom*, the Hebrew word for peace, shalom. Shalom shares a common origin with the word *shalem*, which means healthy, or whole.

Here again we see the interrelatedness of mind, spirit, and body. Together these words give us a beautiful concept of wholeness. (See Numbers 6:24-26, where Moses blended health and wholeness, and Psalm 29:11.) Whenever our physical body systems are in harmony—in dynamic equilibrium, at peace—we are physically healthy. Whenever peace permeates our spirits, minds, and emotions, we can experience well-being even in the midst of turmoil.

With shalom comes composure, confidence, equilibrium, perspective, health, and overall well-being. Shalom conveys rich implication of soundness and wholeness. Shalom speaks of the full integration of life found only by living in harmony with the God who created us and the world of which we are a part.

Clearly the Bible teaches a wholistic view of persons and personhood. It teaches that health is possible only when our entire beings—in their physical, spiritual, and emotional dimensions—are in harmony with both our internal and external environments. It also should be apparent that those whose life and health are rooted in the Creator can experience a wholeness that eludes those who do not acknowledge the spiritual dimension or simply perceive it as some vague life-force.

Holism, Wholism, or Status Quo

People like Richard Young and Granger Westberg were pioneering clergy-physician teamwork and the reunifications of body, mind, and spirit long before the current enthusiasm for wholeness and fitness developed.

Norman Cousins, former editor of *Saturday Review*, termed this enthusiasm "the holistic health explosion." He believed that the holistic health movement developed into a national movement for these reasons.

1. People have become aware that modern drugs are not simply lifesavers; "they can be dangerous."

2. While the importance of nutrition has been underemphasized in medical schools, books on nutrition have been outselling everything but the Bible.

3. Overspecialization and increased use of technology have resulted in a fantastic increase in medical costs and have contributed in a major way to the depersonalization of medical care. Most of all, increased expenditures have not bought us health, only more sophisticated disease treatment.

4. Even though the supply of physicians has increased, fees have not stabilized. The rebirth of family practice is beginning to ameliorate the shortage of physicians in smaller and rural communities, but the inner-city medical needs are not being met. Physicians are criticized for seeking the big incomes that metropolitan centers and affluent suburbs make possible.

5. North Americans are able to inform themselves about health matters to a greater extent than before. They no longer accept medical decisions without question.

6. New interest in the powers of the mind has developed. The biofeedback movement, the interest in relaxation and meditation techniques, the fascinating developments in the area of therapeutic touch, and in imagery in cancer therapy, are all facets of this interest. There is undeniable evidence

that the human mind can be trained to play an important part both in preventing disease and in overcoming it when it occurs.[2]

Alongside the growth of the holistic health movement, and in some cases a part of it, has been the tremendous rise in the interest in physical fitness. We have not only awakened to the fact that our sedentary lifestyle is killing us prematurely, we have also rediscovered how enjoyable it is to feel fit and well. The fitness boom, the lowered rate of adult cigarette smoking, and the greater consciousness of the roles of diet and hypertension in heart disease have all combined in North America to reduce the death rate from heart disease.

We also are taking seriously the experts' estimate that 85 percent of cancer cases are due to preventable causes, such as diet, environment, smoking, and alcohol use. This awareness may eventually enable us to reverse the rising cancer death rate. The surprisingly better cancer statistics among Seventh-Day Adventists, for example, demonstrate how healthy lifestyles can affect one's illness rate and longevity.

You will note that this section refers to the *holistic* health movement, whereas most of this chapter uses the term *wholistic*. Although holistic is the proper term, the word wholistic was adopted by Granger Westberg to identify the Christian character of the movement he was calling for and to distinguish it from the popular holistic movement. Thus wholistic is used to identify the concept more closely with wholeness as we find it in the Bible and in Christian thought and literature. The holistic and wholistic movements came into being for many of the same reasons. However, in philosophy and method the two movements are different.

The holistic movement approach is basically nontraditional and borrows heavily from Eastern religions and sometimes from the occult. The wholistic approach, in contrast, is built on the assumption that there is a God who is personal, transcendent, and involved in the world he has created. The wholistic approach does not hold that the answer to overmedication is no medication at all or that the answer to "overmedicalization" is to refuse to work with physicians or to use any standard medical knowledge.

The wholistic approach attempts rather to work within the system and bring about needed change. Its adherents believe that the meditation most needed is meditation on the Bible. They hold that the best way to deal with the disease-producing stresses of modern life is through the development of a true, mature Christian faith and the practice of the life of wholeness that the Bible affirms. Since identification with the Christian faith and message is important, generally the term wholistic will be used in this book.

We should not leave the description of the current scene without acknowledging that although the biomedical and mechanistic view of humankind, disease, health, and the body remains entrenched, remarkable changes have occurred. One example is styles and techniques of childbirth. Those who fought for family-centered childbirth in the fifties and sixties were overwhelmed by the rapidity of change in the 1970s. More modifications continue in response to popular demand. (Some fundamental ones are inevitable due to economic realities alone.) The women's health movement, the self-care movement, and the overall demystification of the medical establishment are evidence of current changes.[3]

Universality and Wholeness

It is important that we not treat the idea of wholeness purely, or even primarily, in individualistic terms. We must not discuss wholeness as though the well-being of ourselves or those closest to us were all that mattered. We must consider the wholeness of our neighbors, which ultimately includes all of humanity. We are not whole if we do not care for their brokenness.

Personal and corporate well-being are clearly connected throughout the Scriptures. Old Testament faith knows nothing, in any situation or at any time, of a religious individualism which grants a person private relationship with God unconnected with the community either in its roots, its realization, or its goal.[4]

Similarly, the New Testament does not give place to rugged individualism in the life of faith. Note Luke's account of Jesus' encounter with the lawyer who wanted to know how to obtain eternal life (Luke 10:25-37). Jesus' response to the lawyer, which included the parable of the good Samaritan, suggests we cannot realize—now or in the future—our potential as bearers of God's image when indifference or hostility predominates. Note also, in Paul's letter to the Ephesians, that the church's vocation is tied to the divine agenda for the cosmos. This agenda provides the backdrop for personal reconciliation, liberation, and wholeness in the church.

What are the implications here? In our search for wholeness we cannot limit our concern to ourselves and our friends. We must consider the effects our efforts toward personal wholeness will have on others as well, and relate our well-being to theirs.

The point is that we must be wary of implicitly affirming the gross individualism of Western culture. So, for example, in the area of nutrition we must look at the effect of our consumption patterns on global nutrition. Or when thinking about sexuality, we must affirm that both male *and* female fully bear the image of God.

A Christian Response

The purpose of this volume is not just to raise our awareness, not just to encourage new attitudes toward our bodies and the body-mind-spirit interaction. It is to also stimulate activity, to get us moving physically, mentally, and spiritually. We can help ourselves to better individual, collective, and even congregational health if we do so. We should become active in the pursuit of wholeness because it is the right thing to do, because it is the Christian thing to do, not just because it is a trend or a national imperative.

We must recognize that God is the God of beings who are physical, emotional, and spiritual. Physical discipline can have positive spiritual benefits. A healthy body aids in maintaining mental health and vice versa. Physical exercise is one of the most effective relaxants and antidepressants known. Our Christian educational institutions should seek to develop the whole person, with equal emphasis on body, spirit, and mind.

The church is the self-manifestation of the crucified and risen Jesus Christ to all powers, all things, all people. "For his own sake" and "with his own self" he fills the church in order to reach all creatures. The church is proof and manifestation of the living Christ "enthroned at God's right hand in the heavens" (Eph. 1:20). The church shows the authority and strength which was given to Christ to live and make alive. The church demonstrates Christ's presence on earth.[5]

So the church struggles for the wholeness of itself and of the world. And the church experiences the seeming contradiction Jesus spoke of, "If anyone would come after me, he must deny himself and take up his cross and follow me. For whoever wants to save his life will lose it, but whoever loses his life for me and for the gospel will save it" (Mark 8:34-35).

Questions

What does the Bible teach about health behavior?

How did Jesus live "wellness/wholeness"?

How do you react to the idea that wellness/wholeness should be pursued because it is the right thing to do?

In what ways do you try to stem the tide of individualism?

How have your health behaviors changed since childhood? Why?

Activity

Do the assessment exercise 1 in the appendix. What did you learn?

2

The Body, God's Temple

Christianity is not supposed to be simply a religion of the spirit. Christian faith encompasses all a person is—body, mind, and spirit. Yet somewhere along the line the body was severed from the human "trinity." The flesh was viewed as the source of evil. Faith stands in grave danger of being whittled down to an isolated spiritual exercise, with body and mind cut away.

The biblical language speaks to the contrary. "Do you not know that your body is a temple of the Holy Spirit, who is in you, whom you have received from God? You are not your own; you were bought at a price. Therefore honor God with your body" (1 Cor. 6:19-20).

Christian faith is an embodied faith. The body of each Christian is a temple of God, a place where God dwells. Similarly, men and women of faith form the body of Christ. Individually and corporately we are the dwelling place of God here on earth, the continuing incarnation of the Spirit. The Word—the life-giving, ordering, and supporting power of God—became flesh and blood in Jesus Christ. The word continues to take on flesh and blood as persons offer their bodies—not simply their souls—to God in faithfully living out the Christian way.

Body and Self

To say that we offer our bodies is to say that we offer ourselves.

> Since the work of Wheeler Robinson in Hebrew psychology in the 1920s, it has been widely recognized that the Greek distinction between body and soul has no support in biblical theology. . . . For the Hebrews a person's soul is in his flesh, in his eyes and ears, hands and feet, liver and heart, blood and breath, in short, in all his members and senses. . . . The Hebrew idea of personality is an animated body, not an incarnated soul.[1]

The true self is not the disembodied soul but the spirit-filled body. It is the true self, the whole person, that is offered to God as "spiritual worship" (Rom. 12:1). Faith is more than a spiritual concern. It is the exercise of all that we are, in relationship with God.

However, in much of the history of the Christian faith, there has been a tendency to ignore, if not to belittle, the body—the earthy expression of who we are. There has been a tendency to flee to a more spiritual sphere away from the sweat and smell of daily problems, away from the persons who stand in the way of our becoming better Christians, away from ourselves and the temptations that come to us because we are human.

Then when religion becomes dull and routine, the Spirit is called on to mix some mystical magic into the monotony. Someone has dubbed this "carbonated religion." We want to focus on concerns of the spirit and avoid matters of the body. Behind this tendency is the feeling that what is of the spirit is ultimately good, while what is of the flesh is bad.

The church often seems to espouse the view that each of us would be on an expressway to heaven if it were only possible to take a detour around one's body. Three attitudes stemming from a faith that devalues the body or does not take it seriously as an integral part of the person are (1) extreme individualism; (2) fear and denial of sexuality; and (3) the divorce of "body care" from ethical concern. In these cases we are saying, "What I do with my body does not really matter; what I do to or with my body has little effect on my mind or my spirit or on others."

The Body and Creation

For evidence against these invalid beliefs, let's look at several traditional Christian concepts. The first is *creation*. We read in Genesis that the dust of the earth was brought to life by the breath of God. Adam and all humanity that followed are bodily creatures who come from dust and return to dust. Thus we are a part of nature. We are not soul and spirit and mind warring against body and nature, for we were created as single units.

We deny this fundamental unity of creation when we abuse our bodies as though it will not affect our personalities. Stuffing ourselves at meals, neglecting to exercise our bodies, skipping sleep and meals in favor of working long hours, ignoring information about nutrition, discounting our aches and pains—in all these ways and more we violate the creation of God. The care of our bodies is as crucial as the care of our souls; the two cannot be separated. We are multidimensional persons—bodies and souls. We are embodied spirit; we are spiritual flesh.

Creation tells us that our bodies are good, not evil. There is no denying that sin has become part of the picture, but sin does not relegate our bodies to the trash heap while leaving our spirits untouched. The forces of evil do torment us, and we fight the battle with both spirit and body. The same was true of Jesus, who, as a human among humans, was tempted just as we are.

The Body and Incarnation

A second helpful Christian concept is *incarnation*. The Word became flesh and blood—walking where we walk, thinking as we think, feeling as we feel. Jesus was God-with-us, Emmanuel.

Incarnation does not end with Jesus. Corporately, Christians are the body of Christ. This is more than an affirmation of a mystical union; it is a statement with practical implications. We are the eyes of God on earth, seeing both beauty and destruction. We are the arms that embrace, the hands that hold. We are the lips that speak good news, the lungs that laugh with those who laugh, and the hearts that ache for those in distress. We are the body of Christ, the place where God dwells most fully.

Individually, we are each an incarnation of God's Spirit. We are tempted to deny that I can be "Jesus" for you or that you can be "Jesus" for me—that we can be the embodiment of God for each other. Our urge to deny our ability to incarnate God for each other comes not so much from humility or fear of usurping the place of the historical Jesus, but from seeing the Jesus of the Gospels as other than human.

It does not take much imagination to realize that Jesus took care of his body. Walking long, hot, rocky miles throughout Palestine was not for the obese and out-of-shape. He needed and took time to get away from everything and recuperate. Schedules could not be so full of worthwhile endeavors that there was no time for children, for fishing, or for a wedding party.

Someone has said that Christian believers think they are
doing God a favor when they wear out their bodies seemingly for the sake of the gospel. Looking more like tombs
than temples, these bedraggled bodies are offered as proof
of sacrificial service. However, is this what God desires? Not
if creation and incarnation both say that the body is good, a
valuable resource to be cared for as the primary vehicle for
carrying out the still unfinished earthly ministry of Jesus.

The Body and Salvation

How ironic that the church often creates the impression
of *salvation* as a means to save the soul from the damage
done to it by the body. Rather than an integrating force, salvation has become a disintegrating one. But according to the
biblical witness the movement of God is to bring together
into a harmonious whole that which has been pulled apart.
From the pictures of the peaceable kingdom in Isaiah to
Paul's statement in Ephesians 1:10 that it will be God's good
pleasure "to bring all things in heaven and on earth together
under one head, even Christ," salvation is portrayed as a
restoration of creation.

What is true of creation at large is also true of the human
creature. Salvation is restoration. It is not only our souls that
are saved; it is ourselves. This is more than a spiritual affair.
It is a bodily event as well. And its effects are experienced
now, for salvation is taking place now among those who
commit themselves to Christ.

Paul struggled against those in the early church who saw
God at work only in the spiritual realm. There were people
called Gnostics who argued that one's spirit was united with
God. What one did with the body made little difference.
What one ate, whom one slept with, how one treated the
body, had little or no effect upon one's spiritual state. Paul's
instruction was that the body is important, that it is just as

much a part of the person as the soul and just as valuable. "The body is . . . meant . . . for the Lord, and the Lord for the body" (1 Cor. 6:13). When God moves to save us, the movement is toward us as whole persons.

The Body and Ministry

Ministry is not merely spiritual. It involves all that we are—body, mind, spirit. The Mennonite Church's Out-Spokin' program, which brought together persons for bike hikes, proved again and again that even in an activity as neutral as bicycling, individuals can be drawn together into an experience of community in which Christ is present. The same holds for people who have worked with Mennonite Disaster Service or other Christian relief groups, shouldering the debris of tornado or flood. Through our bodies we come into contact with one another and with God.

The importance of touch to the human spirit is evident in the retarded development of institutionalized infants who have received little cuddling. During his serious illness, Norman Cousins said, he valued "the warmth of human contact" even more than "the offerings of modern science." He quotes a doctor who deplores the fact that the laying on of physicians' hands is being replaced by the laying on of tools.[2] What a pity that persons in the church, who are bonded together by the greatest source of love, often find touching so difficult or eye it with great suspicion.

What can free us to touch one another and to do it in such a way that it becomes a blessing? We have been loved from the beginning and that love has given us bodies for the expression of that love. God's love, in fact, is the breath of life in our bodies. As we know that more fully, we will share it more freely. As we share it in greater freedom, we will know its fullness.

The Body and Discipleship

Linked to the above Christian concepts is that of *discipleship.* Paul wrote,

> Do not offer the parts of your body to sin, as instruments of wickedness, but rather offer yourselves to God, as those who have been brought from death to life; and offer the parts of your body to him as instruments of righteousness. For sin shall not be your master, because you are not under law, but under grace (Rom. 6:13-14).

Our bodies are offered to God for the doing of what is right. Most persons will immediately think of matters relating to justice and to a responsible and compassionate lifestyle. Perhaps that is what we ought to think of first. We are called to put our bodies on the line, to stand beside those who are alone, to walk hand in hand with those whose way is more difficult than ours.

But what happens when we take the command of Paul into two other areas of our lives? The first area has to do with communion with God. Where is God to be found? Though we all know better, we tend to look in "spiritual" places. The instruction of many spiritual masters is that we are to enter ourselves, to get down into our own lives rather than seek to rise above them. There, in our bodies, God will be found. As Paul says more clearly in Galatians 2:20, "Christ lives in me." Because we have been raised from death to life, there is more than the spark of God from creation that flickers within us. Within us is the power of resurrection. Within us is God.

The second area is taking pleasure in our bodies. Paul has much to say about freedom—freedom that is an expression of grace rather than of sin. This freedom includes enjoying ourselves, being confident that in Christ we are okay, knowing that we are beautiful and delighting in that knowledge. When the body is not given its rightful place in the human triad of body, mind, and spirit, sensual pleasures are often viewed as sinful. Enjoying the feel of one's body as it works, stretches, relaxes, or loves is seen as somewhat suspect or narcissistic.

Our senses are a part of God's good creation and the primary ways by which we take in the creation. When we walk in the warm sun, listen to a symphony, smell a rose, eat a good meal, caress a loved one's hand, our senses not only help us to experience what is outside of us; they also put us in touch with ourselves. They help bring us into harmony with the sun, the symphony, the rose, the food, the other person. In the experience of union, there are good feelings.

There are also good feelings when we become one with ourselves—enjoying who we are, the way we look or move, the gifts we have. Knit together in the womb of our mother, the body each of us has is a special creation in which God wants us to delight. By doing so we give glory and thanks to our Creator.

The Body and Resurrection

One final concept that counters the faulty attitude toward the body is *resurrection*. Our present experience of salvation is spoken of as resurrection. As we have seen, that salvation includes the body. When Paul speaks of the final resurrection, or when the gospel writers speak of the resurrection of Jesus, they do not have in mind a disembodied spirit. They are speaking of a new body, somehow continuous with the old one. Now we have natural bodies; then we shall have spiritual bodies (1 Cor. 15:44).

Though we cannot say exactly what having a spiritual body means, it is clear enough that Paul is thinking of more than a soul finally released from the prison of flesh. Even now, says Paul, we are being transformed into the likeness of our Lord (2 Cor. 3:18). The bodies that we are—not the bodies that we have—are being saved.

Biblical Wholeness

It is surprising that the church has failed to affirm and live out the biblical concept of wholeness evident in these central tenets of our faith. A return to the biblical concept of the whole person will put us into a position to receive God's blessing both as individuals and as a corporate body. We are the temple of God both collectively and individually, and we act in both realms.

As each of us takes on individual responsibility to be the body in which Christ dwells, we enhance the larger body of Christ. As the church community assumes its role to enflesh the Spirit, it will strengthen the persons whose bodies make up the larger organism. The Christian faith is for the whole person—spirit, mind, and body—and each of us is called into relationship.   .

Questions

What do you see in Jesus' life that shows his belief in wholeness?

Are there ways in which you attempt to separate your body from your spirit? Your spirit from your body?

What are the signals we are giving our children?

How will changes in your health behavior help to reach personal, group, church, and global goals?

Activity

Write a prayer that demonstrates your understanding of wholeness.

3

Sexuality

Sexuality in the Judeo-Christian Tradition

Sexuality is a much more comprehensive term, with more diffused and symbolic meanings, than the word *sex*, often largely genital in focus. Sexuality is our self-understanding and a way of being in the world as male and female. Sexuality includes our appropriation of attitudes and characteristics that have been culturally defined as masculine and feminine. It involves our notions of displaying affection toward those of the opposite or the same sex. It includes our attitude toward our own bodies and those of others. Sexuality is therefore a very basic aspect of our existence.

Christian traditions have been suspicious of sexuality. Indeed, Christianity is sometimes thought to be antisexual. We need to develop a sound theology of the body, for sexuality is a fundamental, pervasive dimension of personality, far broader than genital activity. We need to recognize that most of our relationships are sexual. We can recognize this even as we affirm that genital sexual relationships are only a small part of male-female interaction, appropriate only in very special settings, at special times, with special persons (partners in marriage). We further need to affirm that our sexuality is a good gift, that our bodies are created good, and that it is not wrong to take pleasure in them.

The two creation narratives in Genesis offer a good place to begin considering the prominent place that sexuality occupies in the Judeo-Christian tradition. The first Genesis narrative (1:1—2:3) is organized around the framework of seven days. The second (2:4-25) concentrates almost entirely on the creation of the human being from "the dust of the ground" and the completion of that creation with the recognition of a helpmate. The climax of the two narratives is not the creation of the earthling (Adam) but the creation of male-female.

We need to note the Old Testament emphasis on male and female as essential elements of humanness. It is remarkable that the focus, especially in the second creation narrative, is on the coming together of male and female. There is no obvious interest in the character of marriage or the procreation of children. Apart from the Song of Songs, nowhere else in the Old Testament is there a similar emphasis on the relationship of male and female that neglects reproduction.

These narratives affirm that the complete human being is sexual. Sexuality is not superfluous to our humanity, nor is it one component among others. Sexuality is our humanity. We are created "male and female"; there is no humanity apart from this contrast and relationship (though we recognize that homosexuality raises complex issues we will not address here).

The Gnostic tradition of the Greek world into which Christianity was born had a very different view of human sexuality, which was widespread. In this tradition sexuality was not understood as the fundamental character of life but as something to be overcome. This attitude was related to the understanding of human life as essentially detached, individual, and isolated. The problem with sexuality was clear:

it makes us dependent on other persons, it gets us involved with them, and it prevents us from "creating" ourselves. This view of personhood, which has crept into the church's message, suggested that the body is evil.

In contrast, the Hebraic message is that sexuality is not an insignificant part of our humanity. It is the decisive mark of our humanity by which we are reminded that we need one another. As sexual beings we are reminded that we do not create ourselves.

The New Testament affirms the body as good, as beautiful, as a magnificent work of God the Creator, as worthy of honor and deserving our conscientious care. In Jesus Christ we have a model for human maturity—which includes maturity in relation to our sexuality. In Jesus we find one who overcame alienation from God, was accepting of himself, was open to the world, and established communion with his fellow human beings through acts of tenderness and strength, of love and service. His relationships with others were invariably positive, rooted in concern for their well-being rather than in anxiety about his own purity. As messenger of the new covenant, Jesus delivered to all humans the promise of God's creating, forgiving, and healing love.

We need to interpret the meaning of our sexuality, our personhood, in the light of that covenant promise. That promise frees us from captivity to the cultural patterns of the past while encouraging us to preserve the divinely established values that informed those patterns.

When we fail to realize the profound sense in which we are bodies, we tend to minimize the personal and spiritual significance of activities that we perform through our bodies—the significance of how we treat our bodies and what we put into them. When we do not consider our bodies as fully us, fully personal, our relationships to other body-persons are diminished. Then we are more likely to sin through our bodies. (For more on this see *Embodiment: An*

Approach to Sexuality and Christian Theology, by John B. Nelson, Augsburg Publishing House, 1978.)

We have begun to become aware of the losses that have resulted from sexual stereotyping, from imposed sexual roles, from the long-held belief that the male is the dominant sex. In the church change is taking place. Yet women are still too often expected to take care of the kitchen duties and to teach the children's Sunday school classes. Women are far from being fully represented in positions of leadership in the church and are still not widely accepted in the pulpit.

Over half the women in the United States today have joined the labor force. Unfortunately, those who choose to stay at home with their children are sometimes made to feel unfulfilled—less than whole—without careers. And "working" women often feel guilty about having less time to spend with their families in exchange for the income and other rewards from their jobs. In addition, for the many working women who continue to shoulder primary responsibility for the care of house and children, there is the strain of trying to be superwomen.

We will not experience wholeness as males and females until both sexes are free to be themselves, until—

• men feel less pressure to achieve, to be macho, and are comfortable in expressing emotion;

• men are able to develop their nurturing capacities;

• women are free to exercise leadership and are valued for their ideas;

• women may develop whatever talents and pursue whatever interests they have.

The revelation in Jesus Christ and the new covenant under him offer some definition of the goals for interpersonal relationships, which should—

• enhance rather than limit the freedom of the individuals involved;

• be vehicles for expressing the love that is commanded

in the New Testament—a compassionate and consistent concern for the well-being of others;

• bolster the creative potential of persons in their task of stewardship of God's world;

• kindle that joy that is one of humankind's chief means of glorifying the Creator;

• open to persons that flow of grace that will enable them to bear their burdens without despair.

If the church is to be the church in our time, then any prophetic leadership it gives must take account of two things—first, the actual problems people face in our contemporary situation; and second, the essential gospel for which the church stands.

The sexual problems today are obvious. But what is the essential gospel as far as it relates to sexuality?

The biblical writings contain a curious mixture of attitudes toward human sexuality. While the overall view in the historical-theological tradition is heavily negative, the thrust of the biblical tradition is affirmative. The Old Testament writings value sexuality as part of God's good creation, to be used rightly and enjoyed.

However, in the Old Testament writings there is also evidence of a double standard in sexual ethics. Deuteronomic laws stressed female virginity before marriage, but there was no such principle for Hebrew men.

This double standard grew out of the Hebraic understanding of reproduction. Unaware of the existence of the ovum, the Hebrews thought that the man alone carried the seed for new life, while the woman merely contributed the place in which that seed could grow and be protected.

The Hebrew man had access to any woman as long as she was not the property of another man; and any child that resulted was legitimately his. In comparison, female sexuality was viewed as inferior since the woman contributed nothing substantial of herself to the new life.

The gospels do not report that Jesus spoke directly on the subject of sexuality, but he certainly stood firmly within the Hebraic tradition. Therefore, although he was critical of the religious legalism in which that tradition had become entangled, he undoubtedly had no arguments with the Hebraic evaluation of sex as good.

Jesus viewed human beings wholistically. This was in contrast to later Christian thought that viewed persons as spirits encumbered with sinful bodies. Jesus met people in their unique situations with understanding and encouraged growth. In his encounters with Mary of Magdala, the Samaritan woman who had five husbands, and others, he was concerned with their movement toward wholeness.

The door to a negative interpretation of sex was opened by the Pauline writings. Some of Paul's comments were understood by later Christians to mean that sex is a hindrance to the spiritual life.

> It is good for a man not to marry. . . . Now to the unmarried and the widows I say: It is good for them to stay unmarried, as I am. But if they cannot control themselves, they should marry, for it is better to marry than to burn with passion (1 Cor. 7:1, 8-9).

Yet Paul himself informs us of the contexts in which his remarks were made.

> What I mean, brothers, is that the time is short. From now on those who have wives should live as if they had none; those who mourn, as if they did not; those who are happy, as if they were not. . . . For this world in its present form is passing away" (1 Cor. 7:29-31).

Furthermore, Paul takes care to separate his own opinion from the commands he understands to be from the Lord (vv.

12, 25). It is inappropriate, then, to derive general rules for life (as many Christians have done in interpreting Paul) from these particularized comments spoken for a time of crisis.

The biblical tradition does not spell out a theology of sex. But we can derive some general principles from the tradition by which to deal with sexuality in contemporary life. First, sexual intimacy when experienced in marriage, within a responsible framework of commitment, has the potential for deepening and enriching the relationship. Sexual expression that grows out of mutual caring brings self-disclosure and intimate knowing of another.

Biblical writers valued this experience enough to use it as a metaphor for the God-humanity relationship. Ezekiel and Hosea referred to Israel as the bride of Yahweh. Paul called the church the bride of Christ.

Second, sexual expression within Christian marriage enhances the relationship if it is experienced in a personal, unexploitive fashion. But sexual intercourse is dishonest and destructive if the relationship between husband and wife is filled with tension. Unless the conflict is resolved openly, verbally, the tensions will only go deeper, and both, though perhaps especially the woman, may feel used. For sexual expression to be really fulfilling, the physical and mental aspects of the personality must be integrated. "Our bodies should say the same thing the rest of our being is saying."[1]

Intimacy

To be sexual is not an option, but an observation of fact. Sexual is not something we have to try to be; sexual is something we are, all of the time. We relate to each other as sexual beings. Sexuality is that broad dimension of our being that defines us forever as male or female. It permeates all we are and all we do. It determines how we view and experience life.

As males and females we were created for relationships—relationships that require communication. Male-female relationships take many forms. Sometimes the relationship is one of friendship, sometimes it is one of courtship, sometimes it is marital, sometimes it is sexual. Sexual intercourse, then, is a special kind of relationship, appropriate in a very special setting. But often we use the phrase "becoming intimate" to refer to this sexual intercourse relationship alone.

What is intimacy? Harold Bauman has defined it this way. "Intimacy is the experience of a close, sustained familiarity with another's inner life; it is to know another person from the inside." True sharing, self-disclosure, warmth, trust, affection, sensitivity, responsibility, mutual understanding and acceptance, to prize someone and to be prized by another—all of these constitute intimacy. And intimacy is the real need of us all. The problem is that so many people define intimacy by only one of its dimensions—sexual intimacy—when the craving for intimacy can be satisfied only by a relationship that is more than just physical.

Masters and Johnson, the noted sex-research team, have conceded that the use of surrogate partners in their sex therapy program had severe limitations. They have concluded that commitment is the "name of the game." When a couple comes to a therapist with a sex problem, neither *individual* is the patient. The *relationship* is the patient. Why have we learned to focus on the relationship? Could it be because the real need is for intimacy?

Studies show that many single women are persuaded "early to bed" because they are willing to barter sexual intercourse. They offer intercourse in exchange for physical closeness, caring, caressing, warmth, affection, being wanted. Could it be that the real need is for intimacy?

A common sexual problem is for a woman to lose sexual desire. The typical complaint is, "He just uses me. I feel like a thing." What she needs and what he needs (though he may not recognize it as such) is intimacy! Intimacy may also often help resolve impotence, a common male sexual problem.

Why do couples lack intimacy in their marriages? Usually because it was never there in the first place. The North American dating style does not foster the development of intimacy. Dating is commonly a game characterized by deceitful role playing, false smiles, the glamour value system. The true worth of a person is not the foundation of the dating system. Our dating takes place in a social milieu that encourages us to experience physical intimacy before experiencing the other dimensions of intimacy which developmentally should precede sexual intimacy. Having sexual intimacy before personal identity is achieved is an emotionally disastrous sequence for young persons.

Why do women complain of sexual disinterest? Because the real need is for authentic intimacy and they never had it. So often the relationship was built on a dance between the "macho" man and the "romantic" woman. The hope that true intimacy will develop in a relationship not founded on it is unlikely to be fulfilled.

Without true intimacy, sexual intercourse is often distancing, not uniting. There are nonsexual friendships that outshine some sexual relationships when it comes to intimacy. Many a sexual relationship in our world amounts to nothing more than mechanical stimulation of genital nerve endings.

True intimacy requires more than communication. It requires commitment, the kind of commitment that keeps the friend or partner present and involved, caring and loving, over time. This kind of intimacy keeps two people together not just when the road is smooth (and the relationship is sensuous) but also when the road is rough. This kind of loving takes time. One cannot fall into it and out of it in rapid succession.

We are created male and female—for relationship. What we all really need are some intimate relationships. Sexual intercourse we can live without; intimacy we cannot live without. Relationship is the fundamental dynamic in our universe: our relationship to God, relationship to self, relationship to each other.

Authentic intimacy is not limited to married people. Sexual (coital) intimacy is only one small part of intimacy in a world that acts as if it is the only thing. We can and should have intimate relationships with persons of both sexes. It is a tragedy that our insecurity about who we are as sexual persons, as individuals and as a society, makes it hard for us to relate intimately with persons of our own sex. In same-sex friendships we have the example of Jesus and the disciple John. In fact, Jesus is a model of true intimacy in all situations. The components of intimacy are the qualities Jesus demonstrated—loyalty, love, warmth, caring, trust, confidentiality, availability, willingness to risk self-disclosure, sensitivity, reliability.

True intimacy costs something. It takes time; consequently we cannot develop true intimacy with many people. True intimacy also requires the surrender of some independence. But when we are altogether independent, we are also very alone.

True intimacy means becoming vulnerable, taking risks, and we are afraid to do so. We are afraid of being rejected. So we continue on our way as we were conditioned and socialized to. Women pretend, manipulate, barter. Men hide behind shields of stoic manhood, sexual superiority, and omniscience.

Coitus is not intimacy but can be a dimension of it. Yet coitus is the only dimension of intimacy many people experience. And when this is true, even this dimension will end in disillusionment, for to burden intercourse with our real need for emotional intimacy is to ask far more of intercourse than it can sustain.

Bill White, writing in the publication of the Ligonier Valley Study Center (Tabletalk) in 1980, said,

> While sexuality—maleness and femaleness—is pervasive in human nature, touching and influencing every aspect of life, our sexual needs must be considered within the context of other important needs. Lasting sexual fulfillment cannot be found apart from, nor can sex be substituted for, action directed toward meeting one's need to know God, one's need for community, or one's need for a meaningful vocation. Possibly this suggests a reason why there is such a preoccupation with sex in our culture. Failing to know God, failing to find real community, and failing to realize a calling through satisfying work, people are desperately trying to fill the vacuum with sex. The frustration and emptiness of men and women who move from excess to excess to perversion in sex, points to a need which cannot be fulfilled by sex alone. . . . Without intimacy, without a sharing of personal worlds, the physical aspects of sex are torn out of their personal context.

What about our friendships? Why can't we have better, freer, more open friendships with people of both sexes? In a study done by *Psychology Today* magazine, 73 percent of respondents believed that friendships with the opposite sex are different from those with one's own sex.

Why? Because society discourages same-sex friendships, and because sexual tensions get in the way in opposite-sex friendships. Too often men regard women as objects of possible sexual conquest. Why does the "sex thing" have to get in the way all the time? Why can't a man and woman have an intimate friendship without being regarded as sexually suspect?

Because we don't understand sex. We don't have our sexuality integrated into who we really are as whole persons—simultaneously body, mind, and spirit. We need to understand what it means to be body-selves, sexual persons. We need to learn how to cherish our sexuality. We need to know the possibilities as well as limitations of our sexuality, to know its parameters and its messages, to know when and how to touch each other lovingly and appropriately, to know how to communicate about sexuality openly and honestly with either sex.

To be sexual—we are. To be intimate—we can be. We can live healthily without coital relationships. What we cannot do without is some kind of mutual sharing of life experiences with someone else.

Questions

What does intimacy mean?

What does intimacy have to do with sex?

Where did you get your attitudes about sexuality? How have they changed since childhood?

How are we helping children to develop healthy attitudes about sexuality?

Activity

Work through section H in exercise 2 of the appendix.

4

Nutrition

If we accept the essential integration of personhood suggested in preceding chapters, then we must take seriously the question of body maintenance. However, that concern must interface with concern for neighbor. And given the interdependence of our world and Jesus' definition of neighbor (Luke 10:25-37), this includes the whole human family.

Culture Affects Food Choices

All cultures have developed patterns of eating that reveal what they believe about food in relation to life as a whole. Some of these patterns reflect physical needs for certain nutrients. The high-calorie meals of our grandparents' generation met the energy needs of people doing physically strenuous work. Other eating habits reflect precautions against food poisoning. The Jewish and Muslim prohibition against eating pork began when pork often carried disease. Psychological factors also affect food choices. Likely almost every hostess or host around the world feels hurt if guests refuse the food she or he considers choice.

Diet is closely related to culture. Most ethnic groups that have remained together upon immigration to North America are known for the foods unique to their background. Most North Americans have changed their diet patterns considerably since the turn of the century. Today's affluent American diet typically includes large amounts of animal protein and fat in the form of meats and dairy products. We eat highly refined flour and sugar in place of bulky carbohydrates, such as whole grains, tubers, fresh fruits and vegetables. More and more we use commercially prepared foods instead of fresh, unprocessed products.

This overnutrition, combined with increasingly sedentary lifestyles, has contributed to health problems akin to the more widely recognized problems of undernutrition. Six of the ten leading causes of death in the United States—heart attack, stroke, arteriosclerosis, cancer, cirrhosis of the liver, and diabetes—are diet-related.

Changes Are Needed

We do not eat enough complex carbohydrates. We eat only half as much grain as our grandparents did early in this century. Instead we eat more fatty foods and refined sugar. The displacement of grains, fresh fruits, and vegetables—foods with complex carbohydrates and naturally occurring sugars—may increase the risks of heart disease, cancer, diabetes, and obesity. Highly processed fruits and vegetables generally are not nutritionally equivalent to the same foods in fresh form. As the degree of processing increases, nutrients usually are removed or altered.

We need to include more fiber in our diets. Fiber found in complex carbohydrate foods, particularly whole grains and unpeeled fruits and vegetables, helps in weight control and tends to reduce the risk of digestive and intestinal problems. Certain fibers (pectin from fruit, guar gum from beans, and the fiber in rolled oats and carrots) are effective in lowering the level of cholesterol in the blood. Cholesterol deposits on the walls of the blood vessels are suspected of playing a role in arteriosclerosis (hardening of the arteries).

Fiber should be included in the diet by eating the food in which it occurs naturally, rather than as an additive to a diet of refined products. Added fiber can reduce the body's absorption of several essential minerals and protein.

We eat too much sugar. Refined sweeteners and honey supply no protein, fat, vitamins, dietary fiber, and practically no minerals. These "empty calories," often added to processed foods, replace more nutritious sources of calories or contribute unneeded calories. The consequences are greater risk of tooth decay, obesity, and other health problems.

We eat too much fat. North American diets contain excessive fat. Among health problems associated with high-fat intake are obesity, diabetes, high blood pressure, gallbladder disease, arthritis, heart disease, and some cancers.

We eat more salt than we need. Most of our diets contain ten times more sodium than the body requires. Sodium occurs in leavening agents, in salt (often used as a preservative in processed foods), and in some other seasonings. High intake of sodium may increase the risk of high blood pressure.

Many Questions About Nutrition Remain

Dietary cholesterol. In the last few years, there has been much in the press about the relationship between dietary cholesterol and heart disease. Cholesterol is a waxy substance found in the bloodstream. The liver usually produces as much as the body needs. A diet high in fat may increase the amount of cholesterol in the blood to an unhealthy level.

Adults should have their cholesterol checked at least once every five years. Scientific understandings of cholesterol and fat interactions are still in process, but at the moment there seems to be a consensus that there are several things to watch for.

An overall cholesterol count of under 200 is considered desirable, but it is also good to know about the different kinds of cholesterol. The HDL is the good kind. The higher the HDL level, the better. The LDL is the bad kind and this count should be kept as low as possible.

Saturated fats (most animal fats, palm oil, coconut oil) raise the serum cholesterol level, the factor associated with heart disease. Polyunsaturated fats (most vegetable oils, fish oils) lower the serum cholesterol level. Mono-unsaturated fats (peanut oil, olive oil) seem to have little or no effect on cholesterol. Exercise has also been shown to be beneficial in maintaining a desirable cholesterol level.

Vitamin and mineral supplements. If we eat a balanced diet of fruits and vegetables, breads and cereals, with some meats and dairy products, we should be able to meet our vitamin and mineral needs.

When supplements are required, the federal government's recommended-daily-allowance percentages are helpful guides to proper dosage. Large doses of vitamins or minerals should never be taken unless required by special conditions, for the risks may be even more serious than results of the deficiencies.

Additives. Additives are used as colors, flavors, preservatives, thickeners, and agents for controlling other physical properties of food. Many additives, of course, are useful and have no harmful effects; however, others are questionable. Becoming a smarter consumer will include learning about additives and reading labels more carefully.[1]

Dieting. At any given time, nearly half of all adult Americans are either on a diet to lose weight or think they ought to be. There are many reasons—including an underlying disease such as diabetes—why people gain excess weight and have trouble losing it. Some of the reasons for overeating are the same as for alcohol and drug abuse—boredom, frustration, habits learned in the family.

But every case of obesity is a matter of taking in more energy (calories) than is used. Weight loss only can occur when the amount of calories taken in is less than the amount of calories used up. For this reason, regular exercise and a meal-planning program are necessary for weight control.

Most of the many diet books and weight-loss gimmicks are worthless; moreover, some are dangerous to the dieter's health. Particularly risky are plans that promise quick weight loss through restricting intake of complex carbohydrates and eating more high-protein and sometimes high-fat foods. These diets cause the kidneys to use water from body tissues and to get rid of the toxic waste products from incompletely burned fats and unused nitrogen from excess protein. There are other negative effects as well.

For some people, losing weight is difficult even when the diet is well balanced nutritionally. The tendency is to go on and off the diet because of the restricted feeling that comes from having the element of choice removed from eating. And the repeated loss and gain of weight from sporadic dieting puts injurious stresses on the body.

Persons who have failed at dieting may want to try behavior modification techniques, which enable the dieter not only to lose weight but to learn new habits of eating to maintain the desired weight. Either alone or in a group, the dieter who applies the principles of behavior modification to restructuring eating habits remains in control of the diet plan. This is more likely to yield successful dieting. In any case, weight reduction is a matter for discussion with a physician.

A Wholistic Approach to Nutrition

In the Bible, God's acts of generosity to God's children, including provision of food, were almost always performed in the context of the community—the tribe, the nation, the world. Realization of this fact should guide all decisions we make about meeting our individual needs. If we are concerned about living wholistically, we need to assess how our food choices affect the nutrition of others.

In the Old Testament story of God providing food for the children of Israel, some of the people gathered extra manna. The incident is an analogy of our own tendencies to overeat, to overdose ourselves with supplements, to search for easy diets. We should recognize that we overconsume God's provisions of food while others go hungry. The apostle Paul makes that connection in 2 Corinthians 8:13-15.

> Our desire is not that others might be relieved while you are hard pressed, but that there might be equality. At the present time your plenty will supply what they need, so that in turn their plenty will supply what you need. Then there will be equality, as it is written: "He that gathered much did not have too much, and he that gathered little did not have too little."

Doris Longacre, in The *More-with-Less Cookbook*, noted the relationship between our nutritional choices and the needs of the world. Her recommendation of a way "of wasting less, eating less, and spending less which gives not less but more" has provided us with a new perspective on food and has led us to see ourselves and our needs as a part of a whole that comprises all of creation.[2]

Longacre's second book, *Living More with Less*, broadens the application of the more-with-less concept. It focuses on five standards that form "a solid, integrated way of living"—do justice, learn from the world community, cherish the natural order, nurture people, and nonconform freely.[3] While each of the standards can be applied to nutrition choices, those calling us to do justice and to nurture people have many implications for us to consider.

Do justice. Hunger and poverty are the outgrowth of injustice, in which we sometimes unknowingly participate.

With a wholistic worldview, can we justify our use of food products made available and inexpensive to us by unjust exploitation of poor workers?

Nurture people. In every culture, people show they care about others by sharing and preparing food. Think of the many types of people with whom Jesus ate. Think of the lives that were changed because he showed his loving care in such situations.

Nutritionists working in hospitals, prisons, and school lunch programs have expressed concern that the increasingly mechanized approach to preparing and serving food—as seen in highly processed and packaged meals served on aluminum foil pans—has a potentially negative effect both nutritionally and psychologically. Wholistic living should keep us in touch with a real world where real people prepare and serve food and we have the pleasure of seeing, smelling, and tasting basic foods.

With ever-increasing use of highly processed and packaged foods, and with more and more families eating meals apart from one another and often away from home, we are developing a pattern with a negative impact on community. Along with fewer meals prepared at home and eaten with the family, our diet today includes more nutritionally deficient snack foods aptly described as "junk food."

Columbia University nutrition educator Joan Gussow has described how this easy availability of food affects our relationship with other people.

> Perhaps the most obvious effect of this food excess is that it makes other people's hunger hard to believe. Faced with the temptations of those brightly-lit aisles, those floor-to-ceiling shelves filled with Pop-Tarts,

Kool-Aid, Cap'n Crunch, and Screaming Yellow
Zonkers, it is hard to remember that in much of the
world millions are thankful for one real meal a day—
each day's meal very like that of the day before; perhaps nothing more than a portion of grain or starchy
tuber, seasoned with vegetables and, with luck, perhaps a scrap of chicken or fish.[4]

Controlled or in Control?

Surely the tremendous changes in our diets in the past
few years would not have taken place if we had not given in
to the lure of advertising, especially on television. In a helpful examination of the role of advertising, Ronald Sider suggests that "in a sense we pay too little attention to advertisements. Most of us think that we ignore them. But in fact they
seep into our unconscious minds. We experience them instead of analyzing them."[5]

Richard Foster reminds us that "the ad writer never intended us to believe those silly commercials, only to desire
the products they advertise. And sure enough we buy, because the commercials accomplish their goal of inflaming
our desire."[6]

Television food ads aimed at children generally do not
promote good nutrition. Certainly such ads do not lead to a
wholistic understanding of the role of food in one's life. Using animation and fantasy, the ads manipulate children to
prefer sweets and snack foods and highly sugared, color-
coated cereals.

The point is not that there is no nutritional value in fast
foods—there is. The issue is what we pay for that nutrition.
The cost of waste, processing, non-nutritional taste en-
hancers, poor dietary habits that may lead to poor health
(requiring expensive medical care) make fast foods a relatively costly source of nutrition.

The point is that what television presents as in our interest regarding food probably is not. The task of television is to produce consumers, not to look out for our well-being and the well-being of our families and communities. And the advertisements are only the last act of the drama of mind control. We are being prepared for the advertisement by everything that precedes it. So let's beware—be aware.

> Father God, we have a beautiful country with green
>   fields and hills and valleys and lakes.
> Our fields grow good crops.
> We always have enough to eat.
>
> Forgive us for taking these gifts for granted.
> Forgive us for wasting things.
> Forgive us for not sharing with others in need.
> Help people in rich countries like ours to care
>   about poorer countries.[7]

Questions

Have you made any changes in your eating habits in the last five years? What? Why?

How does television influence your grocery shopping?

How do your eating practices affect others in the world?

What do your church carry-in suppers say about your faith? Are there any changes you would recommend?

What are the forces in your environment that will attempt to sabotage your efforts to change?

Activity

Work through sections B and C in exercise 2 in the appendix.

Plan a "good nutrition" church supper. Provide copies of recipes for those wanting them.

5

Physical Fitness

Although exercise was an integral part of daily work, exercise for physical fitness is seldom mentioned in the Bible. This does not mean that the Bible negates its value. For example, the description of Moses at the time of his death at an old age—"his eyes were not weak nor his strength gone" (Deut. 34:7)—attaches an importance to physical fitness. And Jesus' healing ministry shows the high value he placed on a healthy body.

Another biblical example seems to put physical fitness into perspective. In his instructions to Timothy to train himself in godliness, Paul noted, "Physical training is of some value, but godliness has value for all things, holding promise for both the present life and the life to come" (1 Tim. 4:8).

Comparing Our Physical Activity with Our Ancestors'

Planning exercise programs for physical fitness is a modern-day, Western phenomenon. For thousands of years, until the Industrial Revolution, most people's everyday living required regular physical activity. Our earliest ancestors were hunters and gatherers. They walked great distances, dug in the ground, and climbed trees. Occasionally they struggled with their prey, then there were the heavy carcasses to carry to the campsite. Probably their hardest physical activity occurred when they were in conflict either with fellow humans or a harsh environment.

Shepherds and farmers represented another pattern of activity. While they no longer walked far from their homes to get food, their routine work required physical exertion. They herded animals, collected fuel, and drew water. They planted, cultivated, and harvested crops.

Until machines began to replace human and animal energy, it was not possible for people to function without a great deal of physical activity. The change from lives full of physical activity to the sedentary lifestyles of millions of people in North America today has been gradual, as increased mechanization, automation, and urbanization have affected our living patterns.

Comparing our lifestyles with our ancestors', we can see why we are often less physically fit than they. We drive instead of walking. We clean our clothes automatically instead of washing them on a scrubboard or in a wringer washer and hanging them out to dry. Many of us no longer garden. We do not need to carry in fuel or water from outdoors.

Because our ancestors performed hard physical labor, it was reasonable for them to be inactive during their leisure time. Those of us whose lives are more sedentary need to use some of our leisure time for exercise. Yet even we whose work involves the least amount of physical activity are likely to sit down and read the paper or watch television when we arrive home. We still tend to associate leisure with rest and inactivity and disregard the greater benefits we would receive from physical exercise.

We Need Exercise

Our feelings of well-being are generally related more to physical condition than to age. We get tired more easily from sitting than from activities that keep our bodies in motion. Indeed, those who are always exhausted without a medical reason need exercise more than people who seldom feel tired. Moreover, the average adult gains one to two pounds each year between the ages of twenty and fifty—a gain that probably could be prevented by an additional ten minutes of brisk walking each day.

Regular exercise contributes to wholeness in many ways. Exercise promotes and safeguards health. It helps our body systems to function more efficiently, maintaining healthy organs and cells, increasing circulation, improving digestion, making us more mentally alert, and ensuring physical stamina. Healthy skin, muscle tone, and strength are aided by exercise. A regular exercise program can help us feel better, look better, sleep better, and work more efficiently.

We Need to Find a Place for Exercise in Our Lifestyles

Despite the many proven benefits of exercise, many of us continue in our sedentary ways. Some studies show that half of the people in our culture do nothing for exercise.

Our society supports inactive lifestyles. Some residential areas do not have sidewalks. Since the corner grocery store is gone, we no longer walk to the store and carry home a sack of groceries every day or two. We chauffeur our children. We no longer exercise as a matter of course. Now we need to work at incorporating exercise into our lives.

Recognizing that the stresses of our society and some of the degenerative diseases which plague the Western world can be alleviated by exercise, more and more people are beginning to find a place in their lives for regular exercise.

Health spas and athletic clubs have become big businesses.

Walking and jogging have become acceptable activities for adults. Not many years ago the only persons seen running along the road were high school and college track-team members. If others went by on foot, we generally assumed that their cars had run out of gas or that they had some other difficulty. This has changed. Running has become common, whether done alone or in one of the popular marathons.

Scientific research shows that cardiovascular health is improved with aerobic exercise (exercise which helps the body use oxygen). Because of this, many people have begun to exercise to lessen their risk of stroke or heart attack.

Others recognize the value of exercise but have not given it a high enough priority to change their sedentary habits. "I'm just too busy to exercise regularly," some people rationalize. "I don't have any place or equipment for exercising." "It might not be good for me now because I'm out of shape." "I'm not athletically inclined." "I'm too tired." "I probably get enough exercise doing my housework." "I'm afraid it will be painful." These excuses reflect a lack of knowledge about the hows and whys of exercise.

Using our bodies helps to prevent physical degeneration. Increased physical activity helps individuals control their weight through increased calorie expenditure, and vigorous exercise tends to suppress one's appetite, especially just after exercising. In addition, exercise helps lower plasma cholesterol and blood pressure levels, producing further potential benefits in cardiovascular disease prevention.

Research studies indicate that people who increase their physical exercise are more likely to adopt other lifestyle habits that further lower cardiovascular risk. They are likely to eat less, cope more effectively with stress, and even quit an established smoking habit."[1]

Three types of exercise are worth considering: (1) aerobic exercise for cardiovascular conditioning and weight control, (2) resistance exercise using weights to develop muscle tone and strength, and (3) flexibility exercises to improve and maintain well-functioning muscles and joints.

However, it is important to have a medical checkup before starting any strenuous exercise program, especially in the following situations: if you are over age thirty-five, if you have not had a physical examination within the past year, if you are overweight, or if you have ever had high blood pressure or any heart problem. Explain to your doctor the type of exercise program you have in mind and ask whether there are any precautions you should take.

Aerobic Exercise

Walking, running, bicycling, handball, basketball, rowing, tennis, cross-country skiing, jumping rope, dancing, swimming, rollerskating, ice skating—each may have an aerobic effect when done with sufficient intensity. The degree of intensity required to bring about the desired effect will vary with age and level of fitness.

It is important to determine the level of exercise that is aerobic for you and to continue to assess that level as your exercise program progresses. After several weeks you may need to increase or change the exercise (from walking to jogging, for example) for it to have aerobic value for you.

Good posture, suppleness, equilibrium, and coordination are also aspects of physical fitness that a complete exercise program should help to develop. Calisthenics, aerobic dancing, yoga exercises, and various sports help to meet one or more of these needs.

Which type of exercise is best for you? Choose a program that you enjoy and that will have the desired effect on your heart and lungs, but which will not overtax you at your present level of fitness. Many people just beginning an exercise program after years of sedentary living find that brisk walking meets the criteria for an aerobic exercise. Walking also helps them reduce stress and anxiety, clears their minds for creative work, and is easy to fit into their daily routines. Some pace walkers move on to jogging when they increase aerobic capacity.

Bicycling is another exercise that can be started slowly and built up as aerobic capacity rises. Those who prefer to exercise at home may jump rope or run in place. Whenever possible, incorporate physical activity into your daily routine. Taking an exercise break at your desk or stretching your arms at a red light can keep muscles toned and flexible.

If you want quick improvement from an exercise program, exercise longer but not harder. Overexercise can lead to muscle loss or injury of muscles, tendons, or joints. Occasionally strenuous and uncustomary activity causes a heart attack in one who unknowingly has arteriosclerosis of the coronary arteries.

Physical Fitness and Wholeness

Exercise is important for our total physical and emotional well-being. Ideally, it places regular but moderate demands on the body and its systems. In a wholistic lifestyle, keeping physically fit also includes developing relationships with other people. This can include playing actively with small children, taking an exercise break with a co-worker, jogging with a neighbor, backpacking with a friend, or bicycling with your family.

Working with your community to establish recreation programs, bicycle paths, neighborhood gardens, and public parks allows you to relate physical fitness to a life of wholeness. Participating in walk-a-thons and bike-a-thons sponsored by church and community organizations to raise money for (and heighten interest in) charitable programs is another way to relate physical fitness to wholistic living.

There are other less direct ways to join our concern for personal fitness with our concern for the well-being of others. Helping disadvantaged persons is one way. Assisting them in home maintenance or repair, for example, begins to meet needs for physical exercise, helps to fill a sustenance or security need of another, and builds relationships.

Finally, a word on gimmicks and gadgets. One of the difficulties in the maintenance of physical fitness is lack of motivation. Too often we look outside ourselves for motivation. This tendency creates the market for all kinds of devices and methods to compensate for our lack of willpower. There are two important issues here: (1) the relation of willpower to wholeness and (2) the just use of economic resources.

Have we moved toward wholeness when we allow ourselves to be dependent on extrinsic motivators? If we rely primarily on external sources of motivation, will we be able to act on the merits of an issue? How does reliance on extrinsic motivators affect the development of those we nurture? Might it make them more susceptible to manipulators that may not have a Christocentric worldview?

Then there is the just use of limited resources. When we buy into fads and gimmicks, we have less money to contribute to peace and justice causes. And we encourage the proliferation of similarly questionable products and programs.

What are the alternatives? One is to identify persons in the community of faith who have the gift of self-discipline and ask them to share their vision. This approach gets at the business of motivation without sacrificing the will to the contrivances of those who might manipulate for profit.

Questions

What do you do for exercise?

How does our fitness or lack thereof affect our ability to love and serve our God?

How can we help each other to be more fit?

What in your family history tells you it is important for you to be thoughtful in this area?

What are the things that make regular exercise difficult for you? How can the church help you?

What benefits from exercise do you want most? Stress management? More energy? Cardiovascular improvement? Strength? Flexibility? General well-being?

What societal norms would be challenged by changing your exercise habits?

Activity

Plan a walk or do some other exercise with someone in your congregation. Use the time for sharing and worship.

6

Mental Health

The Church and Mental Health

Throughout most of recorded history, mental health activity has been carried out by religious institutions and individuals within religious communities. For thousands of years, priests, witch doctors, oracles, shamans, and ministers have helped people to cope with problems in living. Only in relatively recent times have mental health professionals assumed the role of helping individuals with psychological problems.

Mental health and mental illness are contemporary labels for a centuries-old concern of the church for the healing of persons. Although it has been designated by various labels, the concern goes back to Jesus of Nazareth and before that to the wise leaders and spiritual guides of Israel. Ministers have within their professional identity a long tradition of healing the broken spirits of the people. A great pastoral counselor of the fourth century referred to himself and fellow clergy as "physicians of the soul."

As members of the oldest counseling and helping profession, ministers have a rich heritage to draw from for their work with troubled people. To this heritage have now been added the contemporary insights about human nature from the social and behavioral sciences and the new skills from the counseling and psychotherapeutic disciplines. The convergence of these new streams with the age-old stream of concern about mental and spiritual health has produced the current flowering of the church's interest in mental health.

The church has an inescapable responsibility in mental health because of its natural interest in eliminating human pain wherever it exists. Christian love includes the ability to see in mental illness statistics not just numbers but human suffering. If we pass by on the other side, we do so at the price of relevance to the situations in which people endure the pain of guilt, anxiety, and loneliness. The issues then are basic. The spiritual integrity of the church and its relevance to the ills of our society are at stake!

Describing Mental Health

A danger in thinking about wholeness and mental health is doing so in either-or terms. Persons speak about themselves and others as if they were either mentally ill or mentally well. All of us, at all times, are a curious mixture of health and illness. Instead of an either-or approach, it is more useful to think in terms of a continuum, with illness at one end and health at the other.

IllnessHealth

Sometimes we are closer to the health end of the continuum; sometimes we are closer to the illness side. Since we are always in the process of becoming, our location on the continuum will change continually. The Christian message is not an either-or message; rather, it affirms God's presence with us at all times.

Mental health is not an end in itself. In the Sermon on the Mount, Jesus said, "Seek first his kingdom and his righteousness, and all these things will be given to you as well" (Matt. 6:33). The most important thing from a Christian standpoint is obedience to God. When obedience is central, other aspects of life are seen in their proper perspective.

The model prayer of Jesus contains a petition for daily bread and the ability to forgive those who have wronged us. Neither physical nor social needs are denied. But they are not mentioned until after the plea for the kingdom of God to become a reality on earth. Mental health, therefore, is a by-product of surrender to values higher than ourselves. Mental health is related to our outlook on life. For the Christian the important question is this: What can I offer to others? A person who contributes to the well-being of others experiences a greater degree of mental health.

Mental health is more than satisfactory adjustment in society, more than simply coping with life as it is. There is a danger in regarding mental health as synonymous with adjustment to reality, to society, to other people. The danger is that authentic or healthy persons will be defined not in their own right, not according to their commitment to others, but rather in environmentally centered terms. The Bible contains many portraits of people who did not adjust to their environment, to situations as they were. These persons operated out of a sense of obedience to God and experienced a wellness, a wholeness, a holiness more in keeping with the Christian understanding of mental health.

Most people do not associate holiness with health. Originally the word *holy* described a person who was healthy, mature, full of interest in others, brimming with physical and spiritual vitality. Holy comes from an Old English word that meant healthy or whole, as compared to being ill—physically, mentally, or emotionally.

A link between holiness and health is suggested in the

two greatest commandments. "Love the Lord your God with all your heart and with all your soul and with all your mind and with all your strength. . . . Love your neighbor as yourself" (Mark 12:30-31).

A holy person, then, is not a self-righteous spoilsport. A holy person is one whose fragmented life is made whole through a restored relationship with God so that mind and heart, body and spirit, are directed in a profound concern toward other people.

Holiness includes physical health, whereby we enjoy all of the sensual pleasures of life including mental vigor, which widens our horizons of understanding; emotional stability, from which we derive a sense of quiet composure even in times of stress; and spiritual "at-one-ment" with God, which enables us to feel at home with ourselves and those around us. Holiness involves the whole person. It is a balance between feeling and intellect, spirit and body, brought about through a genuine relationship with God.

Over the years the issue of mental health has been associated with *feeling*. For many Christians there has been confusion regarding our feelings and what to do with them. An example is anger, which has been particularly troublesome to persons in peace churches because of their stance on war and violence.

Ephesians 4:26-27 is often cited as a prohibition against anger. " 'In your anger do not sin': Do not let the sun go down while you are still angry, and do not give the devil a foothold." However, the issue is not anger. The issue is rather how anger is handled. Fear has led many Christians to deny the existence of seemingly "negative" feelings. The problem is that when such feelings aren't acknowledged, precisely those things we are warned of in Ephesians come to pass. Ephesians and Colossians (3:8) warn us not to let anger fester inside. Instead we are to deal with anger openly so fear can be banished. We experience mental health as we allow God's reality to enter all areas of our lives.

Just as we cannot expect perfection in ourselves, neither should we expect magic in "cures." The biblical material indicates that evil is a flaw running through all creation, not a separate entity which can somehow be destroyed or exorcised. We need to be wary of any technique that promises total relief from the adversity that is a normal part of life.

Wellness, wholeness, and holiness cannot be viewed as the absence of suffering and difficulty. Wholeness has to do with obedience to God, with loving the Lord our God and with loving our neighbors as ourselves. Wholeness includes having a profound concern for other persons.

Jesus invited us to follow him. It is in the following that we experience mental health, wholeness, and holiness. Following involves searching and struggling, falling down, getting up, and going on. Again we see that wholeness and mental health have more to do with outlook on life than with alleviation of difficulty.

In a lecture some years ago, Dr. William C. Menninger of the Menninger Foundation (Kansas) suggested seven criteria for evaluating emotional maturity:

1. The ability to deal with reality—the world in which we live—and with all the hostility that surrounds us. Selfishness, suspicion, lack of understanding, dishonesty, disappointment, loss—these and many more realities make life difficult. Wholeness comes from experiencing the peace that Christ gives us, which provides a reservoir of strength, so that when the going gets rough we don't become excessively nervous and upset.

2. The capacity to adapt to change. Life is a series of changes. We are not the same persons we were last year or even yesterday. Likewise the world in which we live is not the same as the one that existed last year or yesterday.

Wholeness and mental health from a Christian point of view means rising above our environment. Commitment to a way of life will provide a core of stability in the changing world around us to which we must adapt.

3. Being relatively free of symptoms produced by tensions and anxieties. Being able to relax, not having to be the center of attention, relieves anxiety about what is going to happen.

4. The capacity to find more satisfaction in giving than in receiving. Our lives begin with everything coming our way. Gradually the process reverses. As we develop the capacity to give ourselves fully to others, we become more whole.

5. The capacity to relate to other people in a consistent manner with satisfaction and helpfulness. The creation narratives in Genesis suggest we were created to relate to others. Our own completeness is realized when we are in community with others.

6. The capacity to sublimate, to direct hostile energy into creative and constructive outlets. It is unrealistic to think that we will not experience feelings of anger and hostility. It is impossible for us to will away uncomfortable feelings. Needless to say, we sometimes hurt the people around us by lashing out at them. At other times we turn these hostile feelings in on ourselves. When we can channel these hostile energies in useful directions, instead of allowing them to be destructive of ourselves or others, we are on the road to wholeness.

7. The capacity to love. As Christians we nurture this capacity as a result of having first experienced God's care and concern for us. Our wholeness comes, not because we believe that we are obligated to love, but as a response to the love shown to us.

Movement Toward Wholeness

We will maintain our mental health most readily if we give time and effort to nurturing it. Just as the muscles of our bodies need to be exercised, so also our emotional and spiritual sides need attention and exercise. Physical exercise is not a guarantee of perfect health; neither is emotional exercise. Psychologist-priest Henri Nouwen has suggested that there are three movements toward spiritual and emotional wholeness—from loneliness to solitude, from hostility to hospitality, and from illusion to prayer.[1]

Many people seem stuck at the point of loneliness. Loneliness is actually shutting ourselves off from others and from ourselves. On the other hand, it is in solitude, in being alone with ourselves and listening to God's voice, that we receive a measure of wholeness.

Our society seems increasingly filled with fearful, defensive, aggressive people anxiously guarding their property and looking at those around them with suspicion. On the path toward wholeness our hostility and suspicion will turn into hospitality. The calling of all Christians is to offer an open and hospitable space to strangers.

As we move from illusion to prayer, we experience greater wholeness. There are guidelines we can follow in developing a sense of prayer. Contemplative reading of the Word of God, silently listening to the voice of God, and trusting the guidance of a spiritual mentor are important factors in the pilgrimage. Without the Bible, without silent time, and without someone to guide us, finding our way to God is practically impossible.

When we reach out to God and we get rid of the illusions that keep us captive to ourselves and to false gods, we enter into union with God. Then the words of the old pilgrim song, Psalm 121, become ours.

I lift up my eyes to the hills—
    where does my help come from?
My help comes from the Lord,
    the Maker of heaven and earth.

He will not let your foot slip—
  he who watches over you will not slumber;
indeed, he who watches over Israel
  will neither slumber nor sleep.

The Lord watches over you—
  the Lord is your shade at your right hand;
the sun will not harm you by day,
  nor the moon by night.
The Lord will keep you from all harm—

  he will watch over your life;
the Lord will watch over your coming and going
  both now and forevermore.

Questions

Describe your feelings of depression, loneliness, and fear.

What do you need from a friend or pastor when you have those feelings?

What is the role of joy and laughter in the Christian life?

How do others affect your mental health?

Activity

Describe mental health.

Design a series of "exercises" to strengthen your mental health.

7

Stress

Everyone feels hurried, harassed, or pressured at times. Stress seems an inevitable part of modern life. Newspaper reports of studies linking stress to various physical ailments—for example, high blood pressure, heart attack, ulcers, kidney disease—may even add to the problem by causing us to worry about the effects of stress. Most of us would agree that the advice to try to relax a little more is good, but too few of us know how to do it.

What Makes Stress Damaging?

Many situations put demands on our bodies. Some demands are pleasant, some unpleasant. Lifting a heavy package, fighting off an infection, making love, running—all make demands on our bodies, though some are not necessarily experienced as negatively stressful. To understand how some demands on the body can be refreshing while others lead to serious illness and premature death, we have to know a little about what makes some stress damaging.

The word stress refers to the body's reactions to demands put on it. *Stressor* is the word used to designate an activity or situation that makes demands on the body. Some stressors, such as severe burns and disease, cause direct physical damage. However, many stressors do not directly attack us physically. In those cases, the demands made on the body may be minimal and not cause any real damage. What can cause long-term damage and even death is the way we perceive and respond to stressors. The negative emotional response to stress is known to produce negative chemical changes in the body.[1]

A change of job can be exciting and place no great demand on the body, or it can produce panic—a stress response—and, subsequently, severe physical demand. Exercise can help us relax, loosen up muscles, bring needed nutrients to the tissues, and clean out wastes. But exercise is not so helpful when the blood vessels are constricted because of stress and the heart is forced to pump blood against great resistance.

If the negative or extreme stress response is what turns simple demands on the body into life-threatening diseases, we should know what evokes the response. We should also explore why the same stressor evokes a hazardous response in one person and not in another.

In its positive (eustress) dimension, stress adds spice and enthusiasm to life. If there were no stress, we would be like zombies, like machines, never responding to anything. The secret in handling stress is to know our particular stress levels—the point at which we go beyond our more superficial energy level each day and dip into our reserves. Learning to know our own body, our own emotional system, and some antidotes to inescapable stress will help prevent stress from becoming harmful (distress).

Some people feel hemmed in by too many things happening at once—a condition called *hyper*stress. Undoubtedly fewer people feel equally hemmed in by a lack of anything exciting happening—a condition called *hypo*stress. Relief from the alarm and anxiety of hyperstress depends on learning how to turn off the stress response by moving to a state of inactivity. Relief from hypostress depends upon finding a more self-actualizing, involved, and exciting direction in life.

Another important qualification is that for achievement-oriented persons, pleasure is not a relaxing experience. Those of us in this category feel threatened by attaining the very things that ought to make us feel good. Accomplishing our vocational goals, buying the house we dreamed of, retirement, even spending time with interests or people we love, and having sex—all may be making us uneasy. All may be situations in which, for whatever reason, we feel we need to be on guard, even though we are achieving the very things we wanted and have every right to enjoy! This feeling is a stress response.

Our High-Stress Culture

Our society provides us with many stressors. This is not nearly so serious as the fact that our culture encourages us to react to those stressors.

Much importance is attached to working hard, being strong, trying harder, being ambitious, competing, hanging in there, being aggressive, being on the alert for opportunities. But we ascribe little value to relaxing, being carefree, letting our guard down, trusting others, wandering aimlessly in our free time, and taking our time.

Much is said against goofing off, loafing, wasting time, not getting down to business, daydreaming. Less is said against being aggressive, except when it involves breaking the law. The advantages of aggressiveness and a sense of purpose are clearly seen. But taking it easy, meandering, creative daydreaming—these we find hard to justify. Indeed, many find the latter indulgences uncomfortable.

Our culture encourages us to work even at our leisure—to engage in prescribed, structured activities. Unstructured, purposeless leisure is practically a lost art. We are bombarded nightly with distressing news reports and most of our social contacts do not foster relaxation.

Watching television together has replaced sitting on the porch and talking together. The difference is that television keeps stimulation going instead of letting it subside, and television also prevents real communication with one another. Parties are often settings that involve being alert, being on guard. Very little opportunity is provided for letting our guard down, trusting, receiving support from others.

Finally tranquilizers, sedatives, and alcohol are multi-million-dollar industries. Because we have no relaxing activities, chemicals are supposed to relax us.

Means of Reducing Stress

Some stress-reduction methods require formal enrollment or consultation at an established center. In addition, there are now special clinics for people with headache and sleeping problems that do not respond to relaxation programs. Other methods can be learned through books—for example, autogenics, biofeedback, and different forms of meditation. In most cases it is preferable to check the method you choose with a physician to make sure you are proceeding correctly.

All relaxation programs are designed essentially for people suffering from hyperstress, not hypostress. Relaxation programs in the latter case may be detrimental and even dangerous.

Those suffering from hyperstress for whom relaxation techniques work (and they work in almost all cases) still have to go through the day exposed to cultural elements that do not encourage relaxing. Blood pressure and other high-stress symptoms are reduced while a person is practicing a relaxation technique and remain at reduced levels throughout the day. However, within a few days of stopping such a program the gains begin to disappear. Also blood pressure and other symptoms begin to return to previous levels. Maintaining a relaxation program while living and working in a high-stress culture can be difficult.

Stress reduction is only part of the total health picture. And in fact, the other healthful practices discussed in this book—good nutrition, exercise, relationship building, developing a sense of what is of ultimate and eternal value—also help to correct and minimize the harmful physical effects of too much stress.

Individuals suffering from hypostress—a life hemmed in by understimulation and underinvolvements—may want to consult those chapters that deal with human potential and human relationships in order to explore avenues of becoming more involved, finding more excitement or fulfillment in life. Those feeling the brunt of hyperstress might also want to supplement their relaxation program by exploring other directions or aspects of life to see what they may have been missing.

In our highly individualistic and competitive society, our self-images are in constant danger of being damaged. As more and more women take up careers, they will likely become more susceptible to the stress-related ailments men have been subject to.

Theologian Robert McAfee Brown calls humor the eighth gift of the Spirit, a saving grace, which frees us from taking ourselves too seriously. In reducing stress, what is even more helpful than enjoying a good joke is the ability to find the humor in everyday annoyances and mishaps—the clogged drain, the teenager's messy room, the boss' petty demand. Especially beneficial is finding humor in our own quirks and failures. A sense of humor is a matter of seeing things in proper proportion, which means (among other things) having an appropriately modest view of ourselves, since we usually view ourselves with disproportionate immodesty. The saving grace of humor, then, is not only an ability to laugh, but . . . an ability to laugh at ourselves. It involves a willingness to be cut down to size and emerge liberated rather than devastated by the experience.[2]

Conclusion

To reduce stress, we need to develop an appreciation for contemplation. In being able to contemplate and understand God's work in the world, we move from individualism toward community.

Within the Christian tradition there exist practices that foster a contemplative life, including prayer, reflective reading of Scripture, and quietly listening to God's voice. If we routinely take time each day to attend to God's voice, not as an effort to get more done but as a response to being called to wellness, we will experience a closer relationship with our Creator and each other.

Community is a gift of the Spirit that can express itself in many very different ways—in silence as well as words, in listening as well as speaking, in living together as well as in a solitary life, and in many forms of worship. Community is fundamentally a quality of the heart that enables us to unmask the illusions of our competitive society and to recognize each other as brothers and sisters in Christ. As a quality of the heart, community is not bound to any particular institutional form but is free to create new forms of living wherever it manifests itself. Finally, if we keep reminding ourselves that life is full of unfinished business, we may be able to cut our stress in half.

There will never be a time that we will get everything

done that we have planned to do. So here are some practical suggestions for reducing stress.

- Learn to let go.
- Begin listening to what people are saying.
- Do one thing at a time.
- Avoid working all day against deadlines.
- Find a long classic and read it at a leisurely pace; take time to read the Scriptures in a slow and noncompulsive way.
- Remember that the car is not a rocket.
- Learn to interrupt long tasks by taking breaks.
- Be careful not to allow free time to become filled with activities—committee meetings, for example—that are just as much duties as work is. Choose leisure activities that are truly recreational.

Questions

What makes you tense and uptight?

What do you do to manage your stress? How well does it work?

List Scriptures that help you to keep calm and put things in perspective.

What would you like from others when you are stressed?

Discuss the old saying, "It is better to wear out than to rust out."

Activities

Share ideas for quiet times with God.

Work through sections E, F, and G in exercise 2 in the appendix.

8

Deterrents to Wholeness

Throughout history, drugs and other substances have been used in every culture to reduce the effects of suffering or to alter perception of reality. In some cultures, medicine men have used drugs as part of their healing ritual to put themselves in a trance. Certain drugs made from herbs have been used to cure disease or to alleviate pain. Sometimes drugs have been taken to enhance religious experiences. Drugs such as alcohol have been used in many cultures at times of celebration.

A century ago in North America, misuse of drugs—except for alcohol and tobacco—was infrequent. Occasionally someone who had been introduced to a drug by using it as medicine became a habitual user. For almost a generation in the United States, even the use of alcohol was illegal. Many churches included strictures against alcohol among their disciplines.

In recent few decades the picture has changed. Greater availability of an ever-widening variety of drugs has brought the problems of drug abuse to nearly all communities in all parts of North America. All age-groups at all economic levels are affected. Society has become more mobile. Technology has advanced without an accompanying ethic of responsible use. Stress is evident even at an early age. Artificial means to feel better are accepted widely. All these conditions have contributed to the current trend of relying on outside stimuli to alter our perceptions and determine our moods.

These deterrents to a whole life range in effect from a temporary and slight influence to permanent and life-threatening consequences, some of them immediate and some long-term. Deterrents to wholeness common to our culture include (1) legal substances that are produced and used solely for the immediate effects, (2) prescription medicines and over-the-counter drugs, and (3) illegal substances used as "recreational" drugs.

Legal Substances

Alcohol probably has been used longer and by more people than any other drug. Approximately seven of ten adults drink alcohol, and of these about one in ten is an alcoholic.[1]

Alcoholics shorten their lives by about fifteen years. They die with increased incidence from the same causes as nonalcoholics—heart disease, cancer, accidents, and suicide.

John Bertsche, a physician in Normal (Ill.), prepared the following assessment of the problem for a Sunday school class discussion.

Extent of the Problem

Alcohol use and abuse are tremendous social and medical problems in the United States. It is estimated that the cost to society is about seventy billion dollars each year. Some of the more directly emotional and physical effects of alcohol use include—

- more than 25,000 people killed each year in highway accidents;
- 4,000 dead yearly in alcohol-related, non-highway accidents;
- 20,000 crippled or disfigured for life in accidents;
- eighty percent of fire deaths;
- sixty-five percent of drownings;
- thirty percent of suicides;
- sixty-five percent of murders;
- thirty-five percent of assaults;
- sixty percent of child abuse;
- 5,000 babies born each year with effects of fetal alcohol syndrome;
- The primary causes of death in men age twenty-five to forty-four are alcohol related;
- An estimated forty to fifty million people could be fed from the amount of grain used to make alcoholic beverages each year.[2]

Even moderate drinkers may damage their bodies permanently. Alcohol aggravates such diseases as hypertension and heart disease.

As a depressant drug, alcohol affects the nervous system and slows the body's reflexes. Even one drink affects driving ability and could be the difference between an accident and a close call. Alcohol is involved in at least half of the auto fatalities in the United States.

Many psychological problems are associated with alcohol use. Persons unable to handle stress or feelings of inadequacy may drink to become less anxious and worried. Instead of the desired result, they may feel guilty about their increased use of alcohol and thereby create more feelings of stress and inadequacy.

In addition to the huge amount of money spent on the consumption of alcohol, there are the high economic costs

of alcohol abuse. Billions of dollars are spent on job ineffi-
ciency and termination due to alcoholism, medical and welfare support for alcoholics and their families, and repairing
damage to property and treating personal injuries caused by
drunkenness.

Alcoholism affects people in different ways. Elderly people get drunk more quickly than younger people and cannot
clear alcohol from their blood as quickly.

Women tend to hide alcoholism longer than men because of a double standard that judges women more harshly
than men. Women drink primarily to relieve loneliness, in-
feriority feelings, and conflicts about their sex role. A potential problem exists for the baby whose mother drinks, even
moderately, while pregnant. Fetal Alcohol Syndrome (FAS)
denotes prenatal and postnatal deficiencies, abnormalities
of head and face, joint and limb problems, cardiac defects,
delayed development, and mental deficiency caused by the
mother's heavy drinking during pregnancy.

Moderate drinking by pregnant women has been linked
to weight and behavioral deficiencies in their newborn babies. Some researchers believe that hyperactivity and learning disabilities not apparent in newborn infants may result
from the mother's consumption of alcohol during pregnancy. Any consumption of alcohol during pregnancy may be
harmful to the fetus.

Drinking often has a more pronounced effect on teenagers than on adults because teenagers have not developed
psychological tolerance or the ability to compensate for the
effects of alcohol. Because standards of behavior are less
well established in young people, they are more likely to
lose control after drinking. They often have more stresses
due to the new experiences that are part of growing up.
When use of alcohol is added to these stresses, it may become more difficult for the teenager to control feelings or
actions. Alcohol also has a greater effect on young people

because they usually weigh less than adults.

Ten percent of alcohol users become addicted. And because of the complexity of factors that lead to alcoholism, there is no known way of predicting who will become an alcoholic. The effort of some parents to teach their children "responsible drinking" is no guarantee.

It is difficult to argue from the Bible for total abstinence. There are, however, good ethical reasons for abstaining. The Bible is certainly clear on the general principle that not only are we responsible for taking care of our own bodies, but we also have a responsibility to our fellow humans. Some people seem able to handle alcohol, but they may influence others to drink—persons whose body chemistry and psychological makeup are susceptible to alcoholism. And we should be concerned about the stewardship of resources in a malnourished world. Jean Mayer, a Harvard nutritionist, has calculated that "the grain used in one year by the U.S. beverage alcohol industry could feed twenty million hungry people around the world."[3]

Tobacco is another legal drug that is a deterrent to wholeness. There has been an effort to inform the public of the health risks associated with tobacco use; about thirty million Americans have stopped smoking in recent years. One study shows that 85 percent of those who still smoke would like to quit.

Smoking tobacco is the major cause of preventable death in the United States today. Over 300,000 people die prematurely each year as a result of cigarette smoking. Most of these smoking-related deaths are due to heart disease, lung cancer, and emphysema. Other diseases related to smoking are cancers of the larynx, mouth, esophagus, urinary bladder, and pancreas; peptic ulcers; stroke; and peripheral artery disease.

Women who smoke during pregnancy are more likely to have stillbirths and miscarriages. Their babies are more likely to be born prematurely, to be undersized, and to die soon after birth. Smoking mothers who breast-feed their infants have less vitamin C in their milk. Babies whose parents smoke at home have higher rates of pneumonia and bronchitis, and young children have more acute respiratory problems.

Smoking decreases the effect of painkilling and anxiety-reducing drugs. When these medicines are required, larger doses are needed. Smokers need twice as much vitamin C as nonsmokers, because smoking affects the body's ability to utilize this vitamin. Smoking is particularly dangerous for women using oral contraceptives, especially after age thirty-five, because it sharply increases the risk of serious effects on the heart and blood vessels.

Secondhand smoke, which enters the air directly from the burning cigarette, contains higher concentrations of toxic compounds than smoke inhaled by the smoker. These toxic compounds in secondhand smoke affect those in the presence of the smoker as much as they do the person who chooses to smoke.

It is estimated that 10 percent of all hospital and medical costs in the United states are tobacco related. This places an avoidable and unfortunate burden on the high cost of health insurance and tax-supported health programs.

Caffeine—a component of coffee, tea, chocolate, cola beverages, and many over-the-counter drugs—is another legal drug widely used by North Americans. Caffeine is a strong stimulant to the central nervous system and causes a dramatic increase in blood pressure, muscle tension, and secretion of stomach acid. It increases the rate at which oxygen is used by the cells and reduces the amount of oxygen available to the brain.

Some people develop "caffeinism" when they consume excessive amounts of caffeine. This condition causes nervousness, irritability, tremulousness, insomnia, sensory disturbances, increased frequency of urination, frequent loose stools, and gastrointestinal upsets.

Caffeine is an addictive drug, to which heavy users develop a tolerance. When deprived of caffeine for twenty-four hours, even moderate coffee drinkers experience withdrawal symptoms, such as headaches, disorientation, constipation, nausea, sluggishness, depression, and irritability.

Prescription Medicines and Over-the-Counter Drugs

Medicines are manufactured to make people well. Because the drugs they contain are chemicals that can affect us psychologically or physiologically, medicines also can be misused. Drug abuse is the excessive, inappropriate, psychologically or physically dangerous, socially disruptive and/or illegal use of drugs. Drug addiction results from physiological as well as psychological dependence on a drug and causes withdrawal symptoms when the drug is not available.

Sedatives and depressants are drugs that help the user relax. Beginning with the first barbiturate—barbital—introduced as a sedative in 1903, each new depressant drug originally has been thought to be safe but has later been found to be addictive or to have dangerous side effects if not used properly. An overdose of barbiturates, particularly when combined with alcohol, can cause death. The tranquilizer Valium (generic name diazepam), which acts on emotional control centers in the brain to relieve anxiety and muscle tension, has been a widely prescribed drug.

Stimulants are another category of mood manipulators that can be purchased over the counter or by prescription, although some are obtained and used illicitly. One major group of stimulants, amphetamines, are in common use under several trade names—Benzedrine, Dexedrine, Methedrine. They are used medically to relieve fatigue, to control weight, and to elevate mood in depression. People who overuse amphetamines may try to push themselves beyond their normal physical limits, whether in sports, driving a truck, or staying awake to study.

Habitual users are characterized by tenseness, irritability, suspicion, and aggression. Extremely heavy users tend to lose weight, to talk constantly, and eventually to become psychotic. A person who has taken a large dose of amphetamines may become uncontrollably angry and be dangerous to himself and to others.

Illegal Substances

Many of the illegal drugs fall into two basic categories—hallucinogens and narcotics. The best known hallucinogens are marijuana (cannabis) and LSD (lysergic acid diethylamide). Other common hallucinogens are mescaline, psilocybin, and psilocin.

Hallucinogens produce distortions in perception. They may cause users to perceive strange changes in what is sensed or actually to see things that are not there. As the term suggests, the primary effect of the hallucinogens is psychological.

Another serious effect of hallucinogen use is distortion in awareness of self. Users may believe they can float in air or that their body changes shape. This is called depersonalization or dissociation. Mood swings from ecstasy to terror are common. A person's sense of relatedess is impaired, resulting in a feeling of profound isolation.

Narcotics include several legal prescription drugs—morphine, codeine, and paregoric—and the illegal substance heroin. Although useful because of their painkilling effect, the prescription narcotics cause addiction after relatively short use. When this happens, as with heroin, the user develops a tolerance for the drug and requires more of it to get the same effect. If the drug is not available, withdrawal symptoms appear.

Cocaine belongs in neither of the groups listed above. It is a stimulant. "Cocaine has exercised a tremendous allure as a recreational drug that is supposedly nonaddictive; that stimulates and excites the brain, rather than dulling it as many other drugs do."[4] However, this drug has proven to be anything but the innocent, playful substance that such a description leads us to believe.

In the last few years we have learned cocaine is far from harmless. Cocaine is the basis of an illegal worldwide drug distribution business which produces international crime and terror. Cocaine is psychologically addictive and an expensive habit that few can afford for long. Personality disorders, sleeplessness, and loss of appetite are common among users. Antisocial behavior and violence may also be a part of habitual cocaine use.

The problems created for individuals using drugs are only the beginning of the damage done. Rarely does a person use drugs without affecting other people. The sight of a tiny baby struggling to survive the results of drug use by the mother is unforgettable. With the onset of AIDS as a worldwide killer frequently passed on by use of shared drug needles, another set of reasons for concerns about drug abuse has appeared. The disruption to communities of gang-related violence, frequently tied to drug trafficking, and the cost to the nation and the world of this plague is hard to estimate. The list of problems goes on and on.

Most of us do not use cocaine. Perhaps we believe we are untouched by the problems. Do we have any responsibility in this area? What can we do about such problems?

Wholistic Living and Drug Abuse

Almost always those who use drugs of any type do so because they are looking for a way to feel better about themselves. Instead of resisting their search, we need to recognize ways in which our relationship with them can lead all of us to wholistic living.

In some cases, people who have developed a drug dependency may require a treatment program at a drug crisis center, a hospital emergency room, or a mental health center. Friends and family of individuals who need help will want to provide support and understanding. Family members are often encouraged to become involved in the treatment process.

Parents have a unique role in helping children develop a pattern of life that does not require substances to provide temporary highs. How we handle or evade the problems and stresses of everyday life, how we face or avoid challenge, how we meet or dodge our responsibilities—all model (for good or bad) how we approach living.

Parents dependent on alcohol, cigarettes, caffeine, or tranquilizers are handicapped in discussing drug use with their children. They may see the legality or illegality of these substances as the only valid argument. However, only if we adults disapprove of drug abuse in any form will we be able to discuss drug dependence with our children in a productive way.

Dr. Jep Hostetler has written a book, *10 Things Parents Should Know About Drug and Alcohol Abuse*. He gives concrete, practical suggestions to parents on how to talk to children and young people.

As we consider deterrents to wholeness, we need to look at the problem broadly—not casting blame on any segment of society, not making exaggerated, irrational claims regarding the causes and effects, and not stereotyping those who are different from us in appearance or response to life.

Because drug abuse is a social as much as personal problem, we should try to implement changes in social conditions that lead to this problem. War, destruction, and famine
are everyday realities in our world. Our cities bulge with
people whose labor is not needed or who work at jobs without meaning. When advertising and technology offer
glimpses of escape from the boredom or frustration that has
beset us, is it any wonder people seek relief in whatever
drug is acceptable to the segment of society with which they
identify?

Many years ago, the Child Study Association of America
analyzed three common arguments against drug abuse that
have wider implications in assessing basic values.

> The excessive use of drugs is destructive to human
> life. Youngsters will not believe this argument if we
> seem indifferent to other forms of destructiveness.
>
> Drugs reduce the possibility of purposeful action
> and gradually erode the capacity for free choice. Here
> again, young people will doubt the sincerity of this
> concern if we are not alert to the ways in which free-
> dom to make choices is already compromised.
> Choices are limited by prejudice, poverty, unemploy-
> ment, poor education, wars. The older generation has
> the responsibility to show that they care about the
> rights of all people. When we cannot ensure these
> rights, we can at least side with our youngsters, doing
> all we can to push for change. The young need to see
> that we are not giving up on the democratic process,
> that we are involved, persistent and resilient.
>
> Abusing drugs is a way of manipulating reality and
> ourselves. This is an argument that is convincing only
> when we demonstrate to young people that we are op-
> posed to all ways in which one individual manipulates
> another or himself. They will want evidence that we

do not condone treating people, even oneself, as objects to be manipulated for gain or pleasure.[5]

Identifying what are deterrents to wholeness requires that we look at the values and convictions we uphold. For ourselves and our children, the credibility of our warnings about drugs is related to our concern for basic human and spiritual values.

Questions

What drugs do you use? Alcohol? Tobacco? Over the counter? Caffeine? Prescription? Why?

Are there ways in which your life sometimes feels out of control?

How do you handle feelings of boredom, lack of self-respect, or worthlessness?

What message do you send to children or young people in regard to drugs?

How can the church help those with a chemical dependency?

What can the church do to combat misuse and abuse of drugs?

Should drug companies be made to pay for the resulting health care costs?

How can we combat the targeting of minorities and children in advertising?

9

The Global Environment

"You are worthy, our Lord and God, to receive glory and honor and power, for you created all things, and by your will they were created and have their being."
—*Revelation 4:11*

As we attempt to understand our relationship with the rest of creation, we need to recognize and affirm that we are part of God's creation. But we also affirm that God has set the human family apart from the rest of creation.

Then God said, "Let us make humankind in our image, according to our likeness; and let them have dominion over the fish of the sea, and the birds of the air, and over the cattle, and over all the wild animals of the earth, and over every creeping thing that creeps upon the earth" (Gen. 1:26, NRSV).

However, to have dominion over or rule the earth is not, as people often assume, a license to use creation for selfish desires. Rather, we must place this mandate in the context of our being created in the image of God, who values the whole creation. We then are called to be stewards—a theme developed throughout the Bible.

> To call humans "stewards of God" is to claim implicitly that humans are accountable, that is, responsible to God. In giving humans dominion over the earth, God has made them answerable for the way in which they use that dominion. And as far as we know, accountability is unique to humanity."[1]

The dominion-stewardship themes in the Bible culminate in the New Testament with the involvement of God in human creation through the birth of Christ. "Christians should not forget that God 'sent his only begotten Son' because he 'loved the world'—not only us, [hu]mankind. Surely our love and ethic should not be concerned any less with *the world* as a whole!"[2]

Until recently few people in the West recognized our relationship to the rest of creation in this wholistic sense. Preoccupied with the human capacity for materialistic development, we have seen nature as something to be conquered or used, rather than as an integral part of our own existence. We have understood life in linear terms—as a struggle from birth to death against an alien environment. We have not recognized our place in the ecosystem that comprises all of life on this planet.

We are part of many systems. The earth is the ecosystem within which all other ecosystems function. An ecosystem is a community of living organisms, including humans, interacting with one another and with their environment according to well-defined physical and biological laws.

An example of an ecosystem is a lake, in which the plant and animal life interact with each other and their particular environment—including water, air, solar energy, the lake bed. Changes in one element may affect other elements. It is often we humans who upset the balance of an ecosystem. In the case of a lake, industrial waste poured into the water is detrimental to the fish.

In earlier chapters there is a pattern of looking first at ourselves as individuals and then at relationships with our families, communities, world. In looking at the environment and its relation to a wholistic life, we must begin with the larger ecosystem—the world. Then we determine our individual roles in that larger whole.

Environmental Problems

As we look at any of the wide variety of environmental problems that face our world, we must consider the interaction of population and consumption. These problems fall into three broad categories: (1) depletion of nonrenewable resources, (2) destruction of renewable resources, and (3) pollution.

Depletion of Nonrenewable Resources. People used to believe that nature provided an inexhaustible supply of raw material for human use. We thought we needed only to discover where the coal and oil were located and to develop the technology to remove them from the earth. With the tremendous increase in resource use in recent years, we have come to realize these resources are nonrenewable; they are not limitless. Moreover, we are rapidly exhausting the supplies. Within the next fifty years, stringent limitations on the processing of several minerals will be unavoidable.

Nearly all industrial nations import—in many cases from poorer countries—most of the mineral resources on which their economies depend. Many of the mineral resources we now waste in North America could readily be reused. We can extend the useful life of resources through various means of conservation, including the three "R's" of recycling, reusing, and reduced consumption. Most of what we throw away—or try to—could easily be reused, as fuel, compost, or raw material. Whatever it would cost to put these materials back into productivity is many times less than trying to create them from scratch, and the energy savings are considerable as well.

One of the largest uses of nonrenewable resources, both in the United States and Canada, has been in the area of energy. The United States wastes much of the energy it consumes, more than the amount of energy used commercially by two-thirds of the world's population.

As we consider how our use of resources relates to a wholistic lifestyle, we need to assess how our choices as individuals and as communities affect the ecosystem.

Destruction of Renewable Resources. Wood, water, and food are among the renewable resources essential to human functioning. Though continually renewed by natural processes, these resources are unequally distributed. In addition, the processes of renewal are limited. Overuse can destroy the basis for these renewing processes and lead to local or global reduction in the production of resources.

Since the beginning of agriculture, humankind has changed the ecosystem through cultivation. Clearing land for crops or for wood to use as fuel or in construction had little detrimental effect when the people were few and could move to another area when the forest was depleted. Now, however, tree cutting for all uses has dramatically increased. As as result, more and more land is becoming unusable through erosion and resultant flooding or conversion to desert, depending on the climate.

In the poorer countries, almost all of the wood consumed is for cooking and heating. These people will pay high prices for what fuel wood or charcoal they can purchase in the future, or they will need to expend much more effort in collecting wood. In more and more cases they will have to do without.

Water is a renewable resource recycled by natural processes. Water shortages and deterioration of water quality, already serious in some areas, are expected to worsen. Increased demand for water in developing countries will continue because of growing populations. In industrialized countries, competition for the use of water in industry and agriculture will increasingly cause shortages.

The limited availability of both firewood and water will affect the production and preparation of food—another renewable resource becoming scarce as population grows and the availability of arable land decreases.

These are political and economic problems, but they are environmental problems as well. Whatever solution to the problem of hunger we attempt, we must consider the limits to agricultural ecosystems that are determined by natural laws and finite material resources.

An adequate understanding of the world development scene and the challenge of hunger must take into account not only the structural causes of poverty, but also the sustainability of ecological systems. This means that in addressing poverty, we must examine not only such things as the pattern of community growth, but also the fragility and finite character of our ecosystem and the availability of natural resources and their global allocation.

We must examine the justice and sustainability involved in one society (North America), which lives a high-consumption lifestyle while others struggle to survive. The issue of sustainability brings to the fore questions concerning the meaning and goals of the development process. It also suggests the limits of that process.[3]

Pollution. We cannot eliminate matter; we can only shift its form or location. As we increase our use of resources, more and more by-products and waste are released into the environment.

One kind of pollution common around the world is acid

rain. Traveling hundreds of miles with the wind, sulfur dioxide and nitrogen oxides from automobile exhausts and the smokestacks of industrial plants have dramatically increased the acidity of the rain in some areas. Though effects of acid rain are not fully known there is increasing evidence that lakes, rivers, and forests are being damaged.

Acid rain has caused tension between Canada and the United States. The Canadian government, noting damage to its lakes from U.S. pollution, has been more alarmed by the problem than the U.S. government has been. So this controversy has become an example of the effect environmental problems can have on relations between nations.

In addition to acid rain, we have pollution problems due to automobile exhaust and industrial pollution. Some other pollution problems are caused more directly by individuals and families through lifestyle choices. Inadequate solid-waste disposal, residues from household use of chemicals and pesticides, and auto emissions are only a few of the problems that have accompanied Western affluence.

Some of the most obvious effects of pollution—whether from contaminants in air, water, or soil—have been on human health. Respiratory disease, heart and blood disease, cancer, nerve disease, and many types of allergies have been related to pollutants in our environment.

Pollution control, whether by the individual or society, will require identifying pollutants as well as changing systems to lessen polluting effects.

> "We need a blend between the peasant's ecological skill and our contemporary knowledge of what is possible. . . . The answer to the litter problem is not an end to ketchup or grape juice sold in glass bottles, but standard sizes that must be returned and will be refilled by any company. The answer to lung-choking smog in cities is not moving everybody to the countryside, but strong restrictions on private cars and ade-

quate public systems for moving around. We need not give up manufacturing, but we must make ethical choices between factory pollution and human health.[4]

Growth of Population and Consumption

Richard Foster helps us to see our connectedness to the rest of the world in this matter.

> What is our world like? Nations are irreversibly inter-dependent. The United States now imports nearly 50 percent of its vital resources, and exports vast amounts of food and technology. Any national decision any-where sends repercussions throughout the globe. Ready or not, like it or not, we are a married world with no divorce possible.
>
> What is our world like? Our planet is plagued by overpopulation and over-consumption. The net in-crease in world population now stands at about 200,000 a day or seventy-three million per year. No one knows the carrying capacity of our globe but it is likely that we are pushing the limits. Overpopulation is the problem of the third and fourth world; over-consumption is the problem of the West. The average American child this year will consume as much of the world's resources as twenty children born in India. Deliberate and calculated waste is the central aspect of the American economy. We over-eat, over-buy, and over-build, spewing out our toxic wastes upon the earth.[5]

As we begin to look at our environment, more questions become apparent, such as the depletion of the ozone layer, global warming, and the sustainability of the many forms of life. These problems lead us back to our biblical responsibili-ty as stewards of the earth's resources. As we explored eco-system concepts, we saw the importance of maintaining a dynamic balance within the ecosystem process. If we take our stewardship seriously, we will make our choices in light of the way our decisions affect the environment.

Both individual and corporate practices of stewardship are required. We are stewards of the earth's resources, not only as individuals but as members of various groups. Stewardship means we curb our individual greed so that others, including future generations, can share in limited resources.

The late Doris Longacre suggested guidelines for making decisions about the consumption of natural resources.

> Of any course of action, Christians must never ask first, "Is it scientifically possible?" and "Can we pay for it?" When asked first, those are conformed-to-the-world questions. Inquiry tends to stop right there.
>
> "Does it nurture people?" and "Does it protect our environment?" are the conformed-to-God's-image questions. If the answers are yes, the other questions also need to be researched. But the order in which we ask them shows whom and what we serve.[6]

Questions

How do you define stewardship?

What do you see as the major environmental problems in your community?

How is your town/neighborhood working to preserve the planet?

How is your church working to solve these problems?

What does our Christian faith have to do with the amount and kind of trash we throw away?

Activities

Plan positive changes you can begin at the next church social function.

Consider sections L and M in exercise 2 of the appendix.

10

Toward Spiritual Wholeness

Much of our experience excludes other people. We avoid those who are different. East and West, women and men, adults and youth, clergy and laity, management and labor, black and white, rich and poor, no God and God. Not only do we cut off those who are different from us, but we frequently shut out even those close to us.

More and more people live closer and closer together. But are they real people to us, or just faceless bodies? Rubbing elbows with more people has not necessarily made us more sensitive to each other. Instead we seem to have become more distrustful. We seem more fearful of taking the risks of pain and disillusionment that can result from becoming involved with others.

But the rewards of relating are progress toward personal and corporate wholeness. How do we reverse the tendency to isolate ourselves to avoid the relationships for which we were created? Fortunately, God does not demand instant spiritual maturity.

Salvation—remember that we are thinking wholistically —is a process. The scriptural understanding is that we have been saved, we are being saved, and we shall be saved. Salvation is as dynamic as life itself. The waters of baptism are not embalming fluids, intended to preserve us as we are from that time forward. The waters are those of birth. Baptism is a time of new life—a life that comes from God and moves toward God. It is a life of walking with God.

Even the quickest survey of the Bible reveals that the people of God always seem to be beginning. They perpetually find themselves in the dark moving toward the light. This reality is not a justification for failure to live fully in the relationship God intends for us. It is simply the fact of the matter, repeated in story after story.

Such an awareness does not compromise the goal of the spiritual life; throughout Scripture the images God holds before us remain constant. Human struggles do not prompt God to revise divine standards downward, making them more easily reached by the exertion of human effort. In fact, as we shall see later, that would contradict the very nature of salvation. No, the images, the ideals, the lofty calls, reflect the one from whom they issue.

Biblical Call to Spiritual Maturity

The Levitical summons to spiritual maturity is this: "Be holy, because I am holy" (Lev. 11:44-45). The Deuteronomic statement declares, "Love the Lord your God with all your heart and with all your soul and with all your strength" (Deut. 6:5). Those in the Judeo-Christian heritage regard the Ten Commandments as describing the godly life. Typifying the prophets, Micah succinctly formulated the essence of God's call to the children of Israel: "He has told you, O mortal, what is good; and what does the Lord require of you but to do justice, and to love kindness, and to walk humbly with your God?" (6:8, NRSV).

Jesus continued this tradition in his response to the

Pharisees' question concerning the greatest commandment.

> "Love the Lord your God with all your heart and with
> all your soul and with all your mind." This is the first
> and greatest commandment. And the second is like it:
> "Love your neighbor as yourself." All the Law and the
> Prophets hang on these two commandments" (Matt.
> 22:37-40).

The Law and the Prophets were gifts to God's people.
The former was to reveal God, the latter were an encouragement to follow that revelation. Both pointed to God and the
communion God desired with humanity. The failure of Israel, of the disciples, of the early church to accept God's gifts
of instruction and encouragement did not diminish God's
desire for our wholeness.

From the few passages cited, it is clear that the path toward spiritual maturity moves persons into closer and more
loving relationships with one another and with God. In the
Sermon on the Mount, Jesus proclaimed that loving even
our enemies is inextricably bound up with being children of
God (Matt. 5:43-48). To be spiritually mature is to embody
God's love, to continue the incarnation of divine care that
was most fully expressed in Jesus.

A life directed toward wholeness will not be selective in
its expressions. Patience, gentleness, and kindness are
shown toward friend and enemy. Such grace-filled living is
possible only when our spirits are perpetually renewed by
divine love and forgiveness, by continuing and deepening
commitment to God, which we express through worship
and service.

The underlying principle is that to seek spiritual maturity is actually not to seek maturity or wholeness as such—but
to seek God. The psalmist thirsted for God with his whole
being. It was as if he were a deer, tired from a long run, long-

ing for a drink from a cool stream (Ps. 42). So it is with the person who desires salvation. This is not a part-time job, nor is it the pursuit of an impersonal, objective goal. God is the focus of our devotion and affection, and nothing less than all we are, and all we have, is asked of us in this relationship.

Picture of Spiritual Health

Pictures of absolute spiritual health permeate the Bible, from the story of creation to the visions of John in Revelation. To see the fullness of God's salvation and understand the process in which we are now involved, we focus briefly on Paul's letter to the Ephesians.

The vision of *shalom*, or biblical peace, in this epistle has three dimensions. One is cosmic or universal harmony, a restoration of creation. God intends, "when the times will have reached their fulfillment—to bring all things in heaven and on earth together under one head, even Christ" (1:10). Salvation is more than a matter of the heart; it extends far beyond the spiritual welfare of the individual to include everything God has brought into being.

A second dimension is personal relationships. As God draws us together, we relate both to God and to each other. God dwells in our relationships. We "are being built together to become a dwelling in which God lives by his Spirit" (2:22). There would be no shalom, no salvation, without the presence of God in our midst, bringing about harmonious relationships.

But shalom in the universe and among persons is not enough. The third dimension is God's desire that each of us attain "fullness of being, the fullness of God himself" (3:19, NEB). God's hope is that the life of each person will be a well spring of divine love. This is the fulfillment of life toward which God points us.

Thus the goal of the spiritual journey is to be in step with the movement of God toward a final redemption of creation. God is at the center of the picture, drawing all things and persons toward reconciliation and restoration. As persons choosing to be reconciled to God and to pursue spiritual wholeness, we will attain "the whole measure of the fullness of Christ" (4:13). In a word, then, to become whole we are to be "imitators of God . . . [living] a life of love, just as Christ loved us" (5:1).

This is both the goal of the spiritual journey and the path by which the pilgrim walks. We aim toward ultimate shalom, harmonious relationships, a life overflowing with divine love. To make progress toward this goal, we need to follow the way of love and reconciliation.

Gift and Responsibility

All of the New Testament, not only Ephesians, conceives of the Christian as a whole person relating to God, to other persons, and to all creation. And the pervasive biblical understanding is that these are growing, maturing relationships. We are in process.

Before saying more about living in shalom, there are two foundational assumptions that must be made clear. The first is that each dimension of salvation noted above is a gift of God. Ephesians clearly indicates that we are redeemed, restored to our proper place, "in accordance with the riches of God's grace" (1:7). It is by grace that we are saved (2:5). Christ enables us to draw near to one another and become the one new humanity in which God dwells (2:14-18). The unity that we enjoy even now is a gift of the Spirit (4:3).

Salvation—whether cosmic, relational, or individual—is not dependent on the exercise of moral muscle. It is a gift. This is the work of sanctification carried on by God.

Sanctification, particularly as understood in the New Testament, includes more than the usual, limited definition of holiness. It contains an ethical element, thus pointing toward holy *living*, not simply *being* holy.

This then is the second assumption: there is a call to receive and be responsible for the gift of grace freely given. Commitment to God means a desire to walk in step with the Holy Spirit as the Spirit guides us through life. This is the work of discipleship.

Richard Foster has examined the interface of gift and responsibility, or sanctification and discipleship. He notes that "God has given us the Disciplines of the spiritual life as a means of receiving His grace. The Disciplines allow us to place ourselves before God so that He can transform us."[1]

Prayer, study, solitude, service, confession, and worship are means by which we open our lives to be filled by God. It is not by our own power that we change ourselves. However, it is our responsibility to do what we can to respond to God's life, to create space in our lives for the working of God's Spirit.

Spiritual wholeness as presented in the Bible is dynamic, not static. Again, the biblical vision of spiritual wholeness— personal, relational, and cosmic—is not dependent on our mortal imagination for its existence nor on our moral muscle for its fulfillment. It relies solely on God's grace.

However, that grace summons us to give ourselves to the vision of shalom in all its grandeur. Without our absolute abandonment to the call of Jesus to live in the kingdom of God here and now, we miss the ultimate realization of grace. God will not force the kingdom upon us; God simply invites us to walk the way of Jesus toward spiritual wholeness. It is up to us to respond to the invitation.

The question is not, "Do you have God's peace in your heart?" The question is, "Do you have your heart in God's peace? Are you fully committed to the God of all history and all creation, who is now at work to bring history and creation to fulfillment?"

Let us now examine in more detail each of the three facets of spiritual wholeness, noting both the movement that is necessary and the gift-responsibility paradox.

The Individual Dimension

As the individual heart finds its home in the redeeming love of God, peace will fill it. Committed to God and God's plan of salvation, the individual opens his or her life to the power of the Spirit that is at work in the world, providing in such commitment a visible sign of God's reign.

The continued growth of the fundamental commitment may rely on nothing as much as it does upon prayer. Henri Nouwen notes that "a spiritual life without prayer is like the gospel without Christ."[2] The paradox of prayer, he says, is that it requires a serious effort even as it can be received only as a gift. Prayer is a discipline and a grace.

All relationships of intimacy and mutuality require work. No marriage succeeds joyfully when husband and wife take each other for granted. No friendship lasts without a commitment of time and effort on the part of both friends. Prayer is work. It takes time. However, prayer is also the gift of God's relating to us through the spirit.

> There is probably no image that expresses so well the intimacy with God in prayer as the image of God's breath. We are like asthmatic people who are cured of their anxiety. We receive a new breath, a new freedom, a new life. This new life is the divine life of God himself. Prayer, therefore, is God's breathing in us, by which we become part of the intimacy of God's inner life, and by which we are born anew.[3]

Prayer is an integrating force that picks up the fragments of our lives. As we take time to be with God, listening as well as talking, that which is at the very core of our lives is strengthened. The compassion of God for us becomes part of how we view ourselves. And the care God has for the poor becomes our care. The well-being God desires for those whose lives are broken is now our dream for them as well. Attaining the goal of the spiritual life begins to take place in prayer, for prayer is the "first and final movement of the spiritual life."[4]

The Relational Dimension

Spiritual maturity cannot remain a matter of the heart alone. The evidence is strong that even, or perhaps especially, those drawn to a life of solitude and prayer are also in vital contact with other persons.

There may be no better recent example in the Anabaptist churches than the late Doris Longacre, a woman who took ample time for prayer, meditation, and journal writing. From that disciplined time of being alone with God issued profound and prophetic insights, and the sustaining energy that produced the *More-with-Less Cookbook* and, posthumously, *Living More with Less*—books that have touched the lives of many people.

Gifts recognized and received within our relationship with God are used for the good of others. Spiritual maturity is rooted in the heart, but it blossoms and bears fruit in relationships.

The path of spiritual maturity does not lead us away from ourselves or our neighbors. The opposite is the case. In the first instance, the movement is into the depths of our hearts, where we are utterly alone with God. In the second dimension, spiritual development leads us into the very ordinary world of human friendships and human commitments. The horizontal movement is necessary; if we do not love one another, how can we say that we love God (1 John 4:20)?

Through daily experience we come to understand what it means to love, to be patient, to serve, to be kind. Spiritual wholeness means that we will become mature human beings, able to relate to others with the freedom of Christ.

This quality is a "must" in the church. Within the fellowship of believers the two-sided coin of gift and responsibility shines most brightly. Though the unity of the church is a gift of the Spirit, it is our duty to maintain that unity, the peace that binds believer to believer (Eph. 4:3).

Brothers and sisters are not chosen within the church, just as they are not chosen within the biological family. Personal biases and inclinations have no control over the invitation that Christ issues to all to become a part of his church. The growth that takes place within and between persons who would not normally be friends, but who are called by God to be in the same family, is evidence of spiritual maturity. Avoidance of those we dislike will inhibit our growth and is a sign of immaturity. It is also a sign to those who observe the church that the powers of darkness are still at work among those who profess to be united.

The Cosmic Dimension

The third element of the salvation process lies beyond both the individual and the community of commitment. Because God's love is all-encompassing, the work of salvation cannot be contained within the human heart or within close, personal relationships. It embraces persons who are different from us, those who are identified as enemy or outcast. It reaches into all creation, seeking to redeem both the visible and the invisible.

The biblical perspective from which to address all of these concerns is justice. Again Doris Longacre is a fine example. The call to discipleship is not primarily a call to a certain pattern of living, a lifestyle that can be blueprinted and mass-produced. Rather, it is a call to live with Jesus and learn from him how to live. It is a call into community.

Within the community, however, concerns for the poor and the oppressed are bound to surface. So is care for creation. Stripping the earth of its resources to benefit some people at the expense of others is seen by followers of Jesus as far more than an economic or industrial concern. Because it violates the vision of shalom, it is a spiritual matter.

Living More with Less is especially helpful in noting that the development of this dimension of spiritual maturity will be as personal and varied as are the movements within the other two dimensions. Maturity comes slowly and takes work. For some, justice issues may surface when it comes time to fertilize the lawn in the fall. Might that fertilizer be used more profitably by a struggling farmer in a developing country?

For others the issue may arise when taxes are used more for building weapons than for meeting the educational, medical, and nutritional needs of the persons to be protected through defense spending. For some a life of justice means grappling with complex issues like abortion, crime, economic reform, legal and political intervention. For others it will mean a change in eating or entertainment patterns.

In the midst of these many responses, one thing is clear: justice is a Christian concern. Spiritual wholeness includes social consciousness and involvement. Jesus said that when we visit the sick and imprisoned, feed the hungry, and clothe the naked, we are ministering to him (Matt. 25:31-40).

Jesus Is Our Model

Our justice concerns will emerge not from the outside, not by having them laid on us as external agenda, but from within as we identify more and more with Jesus, our model for spiritual wholeness. From the gift of his call to share his ministry will arise our desire and the recognition of our duty to live a life of justice. The gift of Christ's presence will enable us to carry out that call.

Spiritual wholeness cannot be received except as we walk with Jesus Christ, who most fully embodied all three dimensions of God's peace. Our relationship with Christ, our life of faith, is a gift we receive from God. It is a gift we continue to receive in one form or another throughout our lives. Though it is to be enjoyed, it is also something we work at. Salvation does not take place automatically; the path to spiritual health is not always smooth. But whatever the circumstance, we do well to remember that "it is God who works in [us] to will and to act according to his good purpose" (Phil. 2:13).

Questions

What is God's role in your spirituality? What is your role?

What feeds your spirit? Do you schedule time for that regularly?

What part do other people play in your spiritual wellness?

Describe the gift and the responsibility aspects of salvation.

Activity

Design exercises for the development of spiritual strength in the individual dimension, the relational dimension, and the cosmic dimension of life.

11

Responsibility for Wholeness

A powerful portrait of what it means to be real, to be whole, appears in the children's story *The Velveteen Rabbit*. The tale depicts wholeness and well-being as something far greater than the healthy, all-American youthfulness our culture aspires to. We hear the wise old Skin Horse tell the new sawdust-stuffed rabbit,

> "[To become real] takes a long time. That's why it doesn't often happen to people who break easily, or have sharp edges, or who have to be carefully kept. Generally, by the time you are Real, most of your hair has been loved off, and your eyes drop out and you get loose in the joints and very shabby. But these things don't matter at all, because once you are Real you can't be ugly, except to people who don't understand.
>
> "Real . . . is a thing that happens to you. When a child loves you for a long, long time, not just to play with but REALLY loves you, then you become Real."[1]

The Bible tells us that Christ has set us free (Gal. 5:1). The intent of this freedom is to enable us to be real, to be who we are—God's sons and daughters called to accept and demonstrate God's love in our world. It sounds odd to say that Christ has given us the freedom to be who we are, yet that is the good news of the gospel. By accepting and living out Christ's love we become real, or whole. But freedom and responsibility are not opposites.

Freedom, Boundaries, and Direction

A river cannot exist without a riverbed. Freedom cannot exist if not contained within boundaries, if it does not flow in a specific direction. Otherwise freedom dissipates or stagnates. However, the freedom granted to us in the living of our lives is not freedom to do as we please. Our free choices are framed by an earlier choice. Paul knew he was free, for he had devoted his life to Jesus. But he was also Christ's slave; he was a servant of the gospel. Within those boundaries and moving in that direction, he could say,

> Though I am free and belong to no man, I make myself a slave to everyone, to win as many as possible. . . . I have become all things to all men so that by all possible means I might save some. I do all this for the sake of the gospel, that I may share in its blessings (1 Cor. 9:19, 22-23).

Without this understanding of the framework of our freedom, our lifestyle will degenerate into legalism or narcissism. We will either become embroiled in law or enchanted with ourselves. Neither is the way of wholeness. Our primary reason for pursuing a life of wellness must be that by God's grace we are seeking to embody the gospel and to give our lives for that gospel, which addresses every facet of our world.

Spiritual Disciplines

Spiritual disciplines help our pursuit of wholeness. They are an opening to freedom. The person who desires to be free is responsible to help shape that freedom through making certain decisions. Choosing to submit to God's power through these disciplines is one such decision.

Spiritual disciplines can be categorized as inward, outward, and corporate. All three types are necessary for living wholistically. Let's consider one example of each type.

Prayer is an inward discipline without which we cannot hope to be complete persons. No Christian can shirk the duty of prayer and expect to move into close harmony with the purposes of God. Prayer is the "first and final" discipline, for in taking up the responsibility to pray, we are also giving up responsibility.

> If we are to progress in the spiritual walk so that the Disciplines are a blessing and not a curse, we must come to the place in our lives where we can lay down the everlasting burden of needing to manage others. . . . When we genuinely believe inner transformation is God's work and not ours, we can put to rest our passion to set others straight.[2]

We can also put to rest our compulsion to set ourselves straight. For in prayer we open ourselves to God and allow him to do the work. Through God's grace we become Real. We lay aside the responsibility to make it all work out when we pick up the responsibility of prayer.

Simplicity is an outward discipline. "It is an inward reality that results in an outward life-style."[3] Simplicity is not a stark doing without. Rather, it is being of a single mind, having a focused life, not blurred by the profusion of activities and demands that confront us all.

The central point for the Discipline of simplicity is to seek the kingdom of God and the righteousness of His kingdom first—and then everything necessary will come in its proper order. . . . Nothing must come before the kingdom of God, including the desire for a simple life. Simplicity becomes idolatry when it takes precedence over seeking the kingdom.[4]

How do we move toward such simplicity? Richard Foster lists ten "controlling principles for the outward expression of simplicity"—principles to be taken seriously but not to be turned into rigid laws.

1. Buy things for their usefulness rather than their status. . . . [For example,] stop trying to impress people with your clothes and impress them with your life.

2. Reject anything that is producing an addiction in you. Learn to distinguish between a real psychological need . . . and an addiction.

3. Develop a habit of giving things away. . . . Most of us could get rid of half our possessions without any serious sacrifice.

4. Refuse to be propagandized by the custodians of modern gadgetry. . . . Most gadgets are built to break down and wear out and so complicate our lives rather than enhance them. . . . Usually gadgets are an unnecessary drain on the energy resources of the world.

5. Learn to enjoy things without owning them.

6. Develop a deeper appreciation for the creation. Get close to the earth.

7. Look with a healthy skepticism at all "buy now, pay later" schemes. They are a trap and serve to deepen your bondage.

8. Obey Jesus' instructions about plain, honest

speech. . . . Plain speech is difficult because we so seldom live out of the divine Center, so seldom respond
only to heavenly promptings. . . . Søren Kierkegaard
wrote: "If thou art absolutely obedient to God, then
there is no ambiguity in thee and . . . thou art mere
simplicity before God."

9. Reject anything that will breed the oppression
of others. . . . [This] is one of the most difficult and
sensitive issues for twentieth-century Christians to
face, but face it we must. Do we sip our coffee and eat
our bananas at the expense of exploiting Latin American peasants?

10. Shun whatever would distract you from your
main goal.[5]

Obviously the outward practice of this inner reality will
influence many elements of wholeness. Indeed, no part of
our lives is left to itself.

Celebration is a corporate discipline.

In the Old Testament all of the social stipulations of
the year of Jubilee—canceling all debts, releasing
slaves, no planting of crops, returning property to the
original owner—were a celebration of the gracious
provision of God. When the poor receive good news,
when the captives are released, when the blind receive
their sight, when the oppressed are liberated, who
could withhold the shout of Jubilee?. . . Celebration is
central to all the Spiritual Disciplines. Without a joyful
spirit of festivity the Disciplines become dull, death-
breathing tools in the hands of modern Pharisees. Every Discipline should be characterized by carefree gai-
ety and a sense of thanksgiving.[6]

How can we weave such joy and celebration into the fab-
ric of our lives? The practicing of disciplines is one way. As

we open our lives to God, we will be freed of the worries that often beset us. There will be space for a wellspring of divine joy to bubble up. Another step is to focus our minds on those things in life that are true, honorable, just, pure, lovely, and gracious. "The decision to set the mind on the higher things of life is an act of the will."[7] It is a step that each of us can take toward wholeness.

Prayer, simplicity, and celebration are but three of the classical spiritual disciplines. They are spiritual, not in the narrow sense of spirit as opposed to other dimensions of life, but in the broader understanding of spirit as an integrating force. These classical disciplines have been central to the life of the church from its beginnings. They are not to be lightly dismissed when looking at the responsibility each Christian has to lead a life of wholeness.

Which Discipline Is Right for Me?

In addition to the traditional disciplines, there are others we might choose to exercise. (Some will be discussed below.) No one will practice all the disciplines at all times. To look at other disciplines is not to add to an impossibly long list of activities that keep us from focusing on God's kingdom. Rather, we are seeking to find practices that flow with the rhythms of our individual lives and unique relationships with God.

The disciplines are to be a centripetal force, one that draws us toward the heart of our commitment and devotion. They are not to be one more burdensome task that uses up our time and drains our energy, one more distraction forcing us off in some new direction.

One way of appraising a discipline is to ask whether it has a centering effect after it has been practiced for several weeks. Precisely because disciplines are disciplines, they do not come easily or quickly. It takes time to cultivate good habits. But within several weeks we can note some effect. A discipline is worth continuing only if it brings greater freedom, integration, and stillness—if it moves us toward the core of our relationship with God.

What are other disciplines of the Christian life? Physical exercise was discussed in an earlier chapter. Caring for our physical selves is one way we nurture our spiritual selves. Without our awareness that we are body-persons, without our personal commitment to a life of wholeness, this discipline could easily be dismissed as a contemporary fad or an activity for the athletically inclined. The beginning step could be as small as climbing the stairs rather than taking the elevator. No matter what form of physical exercise we choose, disciplined practice of it should stem from a desire to be more fit citizens of the kingdom.

Within each of us the spark of creativity burns. This is part of the divine image breathed into us by our Creator. A discipline that fans this spark will also light our way to God. Thomas Merton was once asked, "How can I learn to pray?" Merton, one of the truly great persons of prayer in our century, replied, "Get a camera and take pictures of small things."

Cultivating friendships and family relationships is another discipline. This may mean writing letters on a regular basis. A certain seminary student set aside early Wednesday morning to keep in touch with family and friends. The pressures families live under are tremendous. Centrifugal forces continually pull family members in different directions. Only a firm resolve and the grace of God will enable a family to discipline itself to spend time together.

Others Help Us

No one can exercise these disciplines for us. However, assuming responsibility to care for ourselves is not to be done in isolation or without assistance from others. We need the help of others. It is up to us to ask for assistance—a request too infrequently made within the church. There are three ways in which our brothers and sisters in the church play vital roles—review, support, and accountability.

The first step in taking on responsibility for wholeness is to *review* our situation, to make a realistic appraisal of our current state of health. The temptation is to rationalize existing problems or to set impossible goals. If we cannot acknowledge where we are, attempting to move toward wholeness will be futile. It will be like giving direction to someone who refuses to admit being lost. The perspective of another person is helpful in making a realistic review and an honest evaluation.

One area of examination might be use of time. Taking up disciplines when our schedules are already full is like writing checks with no money in the bank. Another area might be money. Sharing our financial budgets with trusted friends may enable us to see inconsistencies that our self-interest blinds us to. Disciplines connected to financial stewardship have a firmer base if they are begun with a review of how we are handling money at the time.

The second role others play is *supporting* our decisions and commitments. One dimension of life in which many persons have abdicated responsibility for their well-being is the physical. Doctors and drugstores have become dispensers of health. We may be hard on persons whose car engines burn out because they neglected to check the oil. But many of us think nothing of "running" our bodies without any "lubricant," then expecting the medical profession to right our wrongs. Awareness of our bodies and increased knowledge of how they function will place medical personnel into the rightful position of supportive services rather than saviors.

Whatever the discipline we choose, support is essential. A doctor or nurse may assist us in learning to take care of ourselves so that we can practice preventive medicine. A small group may adopt the discipline of fasting one day a week. A congregation may set aside one night a week for family activities. Friends may applaud a particular sacrifice in time or money. Every dieter knows that a key to success is sympathetic support from friends and family.

The third way others help us use our freedom responsibly is by holding us *accountable*. Disciplines taken on anonymously are almost guaranteed to end in failure and guilt. Just as we need other people to help us set sensible goals and to provide support for us to achieve those goals, we also need others to check with us as we progress toward our goals. Whether these persons are guides with more maturity or peers with whom we have made a covenant, the element of accountability—answering to someone other than ourselves—is crucial. When we fail, forgiveness is there.

Questions

What is freedom?

Compare and contrast the popular concept of fitness and the Christian understanding of wholeness.

Which spiritual disciplines do you practice? What benefits are you aware of?

How do you practice the discipline of celebration? Why?

12

Wholeness Through
the Church

> You are . . . members of God's household, built on the
> foundation of the apostles and prophets, with Christ
> Jesus himself as the chief cornerstone. In him the
> whole building is joined together and rises to become
> a holy temple in the Lord. And in him you too are be-
> ing built together to become a dwelling in which God
> lives by his spirit.
> —*Ephesians 2:19-22*

Life becomes whole in and through the church. No other
group of persons offers the setting for personal growth and
movement toward wholeness in all aspects of life as does
the church. Jesus said, "I have come that they may have life,
and have it to the full" (John 10:10). Abundant life, full life,
is best exemplified and encouraged within the faithful
church. This chapter explores the nature of the church as it
faithfully responds to God, resulting in a place where life
can flourish.

The church is the community of God's people living in solidarity with Jesus Christ. This brief definition contains three vital concepts—the church is a community of deep fellowship; the church is the people of God; the church is one with Jesus Christ, her Lord.[1]

The three elements, held in tension, provide the foundation for our understanding of the ways in which the church builds and encourages wholeness in both personal and corporate life. If basic assumptions about the church are incomplete, so will be our vision of the church's wholeness and the support it provides for pursuing that vision.

The People of God

The people of God are called to be God's family on the basis of divine mercy and loving-kindness. We have no merit that would predispose God to want us as his people. We have no basis to claim peoplehood within God's kingdom except grace, which we receive by faith. "Once you were not a people, but now you are the people of God; once you had not received mercy, but now you have received mercy" (1 Pet. 2:10).

Relying solely on God's mercy and responding to his call are the primary forces that bring and maintain corporate unity and identity. Wholeness in the universal church, as well as in the local congregation at both the personal and corporate levels, is greatly affected by recognition and acceptance of this fundamental fact.

In the local congregation we cannot base our corporate identity primarily on sociological or cultural similarities. For example, while members may share a common ethnic heritage, their shared history dare not be the primary source of identity if they claim to be the church, the people of God.

Family names, shared traditions, cultural customs—all contribute to our perceptions of ourselves. In fact, they may well strengthen the cohesiveness of the congregation. But historical coincidences are not to define and determine associations with the church. To be included or excluded from God's people on the basis of ancestral heritage is a sinful sham. It runs counter to what the Lord of all nations desires. Even in the life of Israel it was the response one made to God, not one's ancestry, that determined whether one belonged: "Let no foreigner who has joined himself to the Lord say, 'The Lord will surely exclude me from his people' " (Isa. 56:3).

The temptation to use ethnic familiarity as a bonding force between Christians has plagued the church from its beginning. Paul continually battled the mistaken notion that boundaries of race and culture determine the shape of the church. "Here there is no Greek or Jew, circumcised or uncircumcised, barbarian, Scythian, slave or free, but Christ is all, and is in all" (Col. 3:11).

The people of God are one people because God is one God. The local congregation, if true to its calling, will do all it can to combat the pernicious power of ethnic pride when that pride tends to limit or define relationships within the church. The healthy church appreciates the ethnic heritages within it, but it draws its identity from God and God alone, and it refuses to allow ethnocentrism to sap its strength.

Of course there are other forces that divide God's people even though they seem to provide common ground on which Christians can come together. Shared economic status is one such force; negative and demeaning attitudes toward women are another. The people of God do not experience the fullness of salvation when they exclude from their awareness the perceptions of God held by the poor or by women.

Racism is also a barrier in the church. When a church that is predominantly white, such as the Mennonite Church in North America, fails to accept the traditions and experiences of members from other racial groups, it fails to receive the full gift of community that God offers. Paul repeatedly stressed that barriers between persons were demolished through the cross.

The church is a new, all-inclusive humanity (Eph. 2:14-16). When the church denies that reality, no matter how subtly, the wholeness that it offers is built on principles of elitism, exclusion, and conformity. The church looks good and true but is neither. Such salvation is fragile and shaky, for it is built on the shifting sands of cultural conditioning, not on the rock of God's gracious call and abundant mercy.

Wholeness Within God's People

There are benefits when members of a congregation base their identity on God's call that they be God's people. Corporate health in the congregation enables the individual member to move toward personal wholeness. The message of acceptance communicated by the congregation provides the necessary context in which members can come to understand and claim their own identities as children of God.

Acceptance cannot be conditioned by similarities of race, sex, economic status, ethnicity, or any other factor and still be the unconditional love with which God draws together God's people. Without this kind of love, the setting necessary for spiritual growth will be absent or severely limited.

A second benefit for God's people is a sense of belonging. In a culture that is highly individualistic, many persons are isolated. Belonging to the people of God brings with it an identity. This identity is not confined to the local congregation but draws on shared stories of faith that span centuries and cultures.

The inclusive power of God's people will not be deterred by ethnic expectations and cultural myths. The congregation that has experienced God's salvation will be able to bring together persons who would not cross paths or be friends in the usual course of events. Jesus and Paul both broke all manner of social customs as they associated with women, dined with Gentiles, and had friends among the poor.

All persons are being called by God to be part of the church. We are called out of our isolation to assemble and share equally in the resources and responsibilities of the group. Old and young, married and single, physically healthy and disabled or handicapped, professionals and laborers—all are called together by God to be the church. The unique perspective of each person is valued. Our personal wholeness is enhanced by being accepted into the diverse people of God.

Nurturing God's Vision for the Church

How can we nurture and actualize the above vision of the church? One way is through worship, which opens us to God in thanksgiving for the opportunity to belong to God's people. In worship we stand empty-handed before the Creator, from whom all good things come. We stand open before the Spirit, who comes to enliven us, to open our eyes to see the world as God sees it and to perceive the persons around us as children held in the luxurious lap of God. "Worship is our responding to the overtures of love from the heart of the Father."[2] And it is clear that God's love is offered to all persons, not merely to our own kind.

We give ourselves humbly to God in worship. In return we continue to receive divine life—life that prompts our worship in the first place. It is this life that binds together the people of God, and it is this life that we hold up when we speak of wholeness within the church. From the divine wellspring of love flows the water of life that nourishes the church. Without opening ourselves to God in worship, we shut ourselves off from the one who has called us to be a people.

A second and related avenue toward personal and corporate wholeness is the practice of silence. In "shared silence" we are deprived of almost every way in which we set ourselves apart from one another. There is no opportunity to compare educational backgrounds, inquire about parents, criticize, tell a better story than one just told, rebut another's opinion, drop names, or jockey for position within a group in other ways. Spending extended time in silence with others forges a bond that words often fail to create and sometimes destroy. This is the experience of many who have been on silent retreats together.

Shared silence emphasizes that we are accepted for who we are, not for what we do or say. Silence forbids self-justification, excuses, and rationalization. The mask of words is stripped from us. Through silence we touch deep reality. We also learn to listen carefully to one another. "The first service that one owes to others in the fellowship consists in listening to them. Just as love to God begins with listening to (God), so the beginning of love for the brethren is learning to listen to them."[3] The practice of silence curbs our impulses to check out one another before we offer the love of God.

The congregation that has learned to share silence comfortably can risk sharing concerns of the heart openly and honestly. To hear others' experiences, especially those quite different from our own, we have initial assurance that our own experience and perspective are also prized. Again this kind of valuing takes shape first of all in silence. It is in silence that our personhood is unconditionally accepted regardless of the types of religious experiences we have had.

Then, in awareness of gracious acceptance, we can share views and experiences without the fear that only one type of experience will be considered valid. Differences are accepted as normal. The truth of God is not limited to the truth of one individual or one community's experience. Rather, the truth of God is seen for what it is—an unimaginably broad and deep love for all persons.

Living as the Body of Christ

If worship, silence, and sharing open us to God and to each other as the people of God, they also lead us to identify with the one who fully embodied God. In solidarity with Jesus, we continue to bring his values and his ministries to bear upon our world. We carry on his life. The biblical metaphor is the body of Christ, a living organism.

This familiar Pauline picture (Rom. 12; 1 Cor. 12; Eph. 4) emphasizes the interaction within the body, the mutual ministry of the members of the body to one another. The human body is a marvelous creation. How different are the many parts and yet how vital each is! An ear is not like an elbow; the heart is not like the stomach; bone cells are not like muscle cells. Yet each belongs and contributes to the functioning whole. So also in the healthy church each member belongs and is crucial to the ongoing life of that body.

To take seriously this understanding of the local congregation is to believe that every member of the fellowship has at least one gift to be in use for the good of that church.

> It is very significant that in each place where the gifts of the Spirit are described in Scripture the emphasis is placed upon the fact that each Christian has at least one. That gift may be lying dormant, inchoate, unused. . . . [But] it is there; for the Holy Spirit makes no exceptions to this basic equipping of each believer.[4]

If members of the body do not know their functions or refuse to perform them, the diagnosis must be that all is not well. And where is there a congregation in which every member can identify the gift he or she was given by God to contribute to the life of the church?

The body of Christ will also be involved in ministry to those outside itself. "Gifts are given by Christ to enable God's family to continue to do those ministries of love which Jesus began to do when He was bodily present in the world."[5]

But until those gifts are identified, demonstrated, accepted by the other members of the body, and integrated into the life function of the body, little ministry will occur. Internal well-being is necessary if the church is to assist its members in personal growth and in serving the kinds of people Jesus served. At the same time, there is a dynamic relationship between the health of the church body and its willingness and ability to minister to the needy as Jesus did.

A healthy church will be involved in service beyond its own walls. And service performed in the name and manner of Jesus nurtures those who minister as well as those to whom they minister. The body of Christ grows sickly if it only feeds itself and keeps a spiritual thermometer in its mouth. To experience the wholeness of salvation, the church must be involved in mission and, at the same time, must actively be discovering the gifts of its individual members—gifts that will be used for internal nurture and external service.

Body Activities

How can a local congregation identify and use its many and varied gifts and integrate them so there is mutual acceptance of those gifts within the body and faithful service in the world? One way is confession. Worship by the people of God will inevitably lead to confession. If we see God rightly, we will see ourselves rightly and realize the need for confession.

However, confession is difficult, "partly because we view the believing community as a fellowship of saints before we see it as a fellowship of sinners. We come to feel that everyone else has advanced so far into holiness that we are isolated and alone in our sin."[6] The church which consciously recognizes itself as a hospital for sinners rather than a hotel for saints eases that difficulty.

Because the church is people, not an institution, it shares the struggles of humanity while it is in the process of being transformed into the likeness of the one who is its head. But if the public facade appears so holy that there is no trace of struggle, no one will risk putting him or herself into the vulnerable position of confessing that all is not well. Confession throws us into the arms of grace over and over again. It must be made clear that the people of God are utterly and eternally dependent on that grace.

Through the experience of confession, forgiveness, and reconciliation, the body is strengthened. This is the perpetual transformation God works within the church. Without confession, growth toward wholeness within the church is practically impossible.

Confession contributes to the continuing work of God in the church and in the world in two ways. The body of Christ becomes more integrated, more whole, and serves more freely. A healthy church is one in which members love and respect one another. When love and respect are lacking, the body is at odds with itself.

Hurt feelings, grudges, repressed anger, cannot be expected to disappear with time. Emotional wounds will not heal magically. A congregation that deals with its hurts and failures openly, honestly, and lovingly will experience reconciliation and demonstrate to others that God is at work bringing unity to all who are committed to divine purposes.

This is an important witness to members within the church as well. A congregation may fail to take seriously impediments to its growth, may assume a laissez-faire attitude toward its problems, or may deal with difficulties in a rigid and demanding manner. Such a congregation will not enable its members to handle their own inner conflicts in a way that promotes growth.

To assume that all in the church have attained a state of holiness requiring no more growth is to take from the church its humanity. Acknowledging that salvation—at both the corporate and personal levels—is a *process*, allows members of Christ's body to be reconciled to each other and to offer who they are to the larger church and world in Jesus' name. This internal work of healing and reconciliation is possible only within the context of love. The community of love is the most important contribution the church can make in providing a setting for continued spiritual growth.

Only a church that experiences reconciliation among its members will move freely into the world as Jesus moved, meeting others on their ground while staying in touch with the central identity of the church. A reconciled congregation will not be as likely to project its needs and wishes on those to whom it ministers. Reconciliation puts a church at peace with itself and frees it from looking to successful results or creative programs for its identity. The church will not need then to demand gratitude or change in behavior as a prerequisite for future assistance.

The flow of grace to the world through the body of Christ takes place only as that body experiences itself as an integrated organism, its various members working together for the common good. Ministry will be stilted or stifled if the internal needs are too great or if the parts are not in harmony. "The task of the Church . . . is first of all genuinely to be the redeemed, messianic community, and secondly to do the works of God and carry on the works of Jesus."[7]

Confession, then, opens the possibilities of dealing gracefully with the realities of the church as members struggle to grow. Through confession and reconciliation the church finds renewed wholeness at personal and corporate levels and is consequently able to move confidently into the world in union with Christ.

To risk confession is to acknowledge that we share a common lot. The opening of our humanity to one another enables transformation to take place and community to be strengthened. We learn that we do hold much in common—from our sins to the gifts of the spirit. That experience of holding things in common was known by the New Testament church as *koinonia*.

Community of the Holy Spirit

"The root idea in koinonia is 'participation in something in which others also participate,' that is conscious sharing with someone else on a continuing basis."[8] This is the community of the Spirit, or the "covenant community," as it has been called by some. Deep-rooted and continuing fellowship characterizes the community of the Spirit. In speaking of the church as the people of God and the body of Christ, our differences are accented. Here the emphasis is on the fact that all that we have is held in common—that is, we are available to others within the community. Wholeness here is noted in mutual aid and fellowship.

Mutual aid in the church has two dimensions—spiritual and material. In fact, "approximately half the New Testament occurrences of koinonia refer to spiritual sharing, and half sharing in material goods."[9] Both dimensions are based squarely on the fact that this community is not dependent on human effort. But where the community exists in a covenantal relationship with God and where a corresponding covenant exists between the members of that community, the movement of the Spirit will provide the impetus for the aid that is necessary.

The primary threat to sharing of spiritual and material gifts within the community is individualism. It is the mind-set that says what I have is mine because I earned it. What I do with what is mine is my business. When we are in charge, the community reflects our desires rather than those of the Spirit, creating a setting in which mutual aid is most difficult. Attempts to help tend to be efforts to influence. Instead of growth, conformity becomes the predominant value. Only as the members of a Christian community willingly entrust themselves to God and to each other will there be the freedom for each individual to grow as God directs.

A significant mark of the community of the Spirit is fellowship. As individualism obstructs mutual aid and support, institutionalism hinders fellowship. The church is an organism. It is also (though not primarily) an institution.

> [The] Church will inevitably manifest some institutional patterns, but no institution can ever be the Church. The Church can never be essentially an institution, even though it will necessarily be institutional in some aspects of its life.[10]

Institutionalization is bad when structures do not allow the church to carry out its mission. Institutionalization is good when the structures allow the people of God to be in fellowship, and to embody the good news.

However, institutions tend to become rigid and inflexible. They perpetuate the status quo, the state of things as they are. Rather than focusing on the renewal of persons through the power of the Spirit, an "institutionalized" church relies on program, technique, and committee meetings. New structures are seen as the primary way to solve problems in a church where the wineskin has become more important than the wine of the gospel.

The congregation that values fellowship makes sure

there is time to relax and play together. It is noteworthy that Richard Foster includes celebration in his list of corporate spiritual disciplines.[11] The seriousness of structures is granted a new perspective as church members have fun together.

The church, caring together, provides the best possible setting for the types of activities that have been highlighted throughout this entire book for movement toward wholeness. In the church we find the greatest support and encouragement for developing all facets of our lives, whether internal, relational, or corporate. The church is the main instrument of God's operation in the world. In and through the church life becomes whole.

Questions

What is the meaning of "community" for the church?
How is your church organized for wholeness?
What differences do you see in the church as 1) people of God, 2) body of Christ, and 3) community of the spirit?
How does your church use silence?

Activity

Plan a wholeness celebration for your congregation.

13

Appendix: Adventures in Wholeness

Goals

The exercises that follow are designed to help people look at their health practices and take steps toward change. Greater awareness is not a sufficient goal. Unless people deliberately plan change, greater well-being for individuals and communities is not likely to occur. Change toward an improved level of well-being or wholeness is the goal of these exercises.

Individual Versus Group

While individuals could complete the exercises alone, ideally a group should meet together regularly to work on them. This aids individual assessment and change by providing opportunities to share findings, receive suggestions and support, and be held accountable by a caring community. The group also has the opportunity to evaluate and change its functioning as a group in relation to various health practices. For example, how well does the group function in its habits of eating together, relating to each other, and responding to world needs?

Groups and communities are made up of individuals. So it is ultimately individual behavior that requires change. However, we must recognize the influence groups exert on individuals. For example, being part of a group means accepting the norms a majority of the group holds. Rejecting those norms jeopardizes our standing in the group. So in these exercises we try to deal with both individual and group behavior.

Leadership

Because the exercises involve group interaction, a leader should facilitate sharing and movement toward goals. Ideally one person should do this for both exercises. Choosing a leader with preparation in interpersonal and group skills will increase the value of the exercises.

---

1. Defining Wholeness

In this exercise the group will develop its own understanding of wholeness. The exercise begins with members defining wellness, a term integral to wholeness. The meaning of wellness is then expanded to include the dimension of wholeness.

Directions

Below is a question to which each member is to respond individually. The leader should then assist the group in sharing and debating the responses. After discussion, the leader should read aloud the material "For Further Discussion" and guide the group in exploring the ideas presented. Finally the leader should help the group write a definition of wholeness and diagram it.

Question

What is wellness? (Circle all the answers you consider correct.)

1. Being free of disease and illness
2. Having good physical health
3. Realizing your potential
4. Being able to reach your goals in life
5. Following a lifestyle that does not cause suffering
6. Leading a life that preserves life and nature
7. Leading a life that improves life and nature
8. Living in community

For Further Discussion

People have long thought of good health as absence of disease. Today persons in the wellness movement suggest health is in a neutral state when disease and illness are not present. Wellness means positive health. Wellness for individuals means feeling good, being full of zest for living, and maximizing health potential. Wellness is not static; individuals can always strive toward higher levels of wellness.

Wellness as described above is individualistic. However, well-being achieved at the expense of others or nature is inappropriate. Furthermore, individualism ignores the fact that God created people to be in community, that people function best in relationship, that the wellness of individuals results from wellness of the whole. Therefore, we should approach wellness as a community concern.

Wholeness, a quality embraced by wellness advocates,

implies wellness is attained when the health of all God's creation is considered simultaneously and when a proper relationship of each to the other is maintained or promoted.

Wholeness suggests that being well involves many aspects of living. It means keeping fit through exercise, proper nutrition, rest, hygiene, and safety precautions. In addition, wholeness means loving ourselves and other people, expressing emotions effectively, building supportive relationships with each other and nature, being clear about purposes in life, and communicating meaningfully with God. It means acknowledging that we are a part of a global community and that our actions have worldwide consequences.

Furthermore, various aspects of wellness are not neatly separated. For example, emotional health affects physical health and vice versa, and nutritional habits reflect global awareness. Achieving wholeness means recognizing that persons are whole beings, rather than several combined parts, and that communities likewise are whole entities.

Many people think wellness or wholeness is chiefly a result of what an organized health-care system offers to people or what they inherited or God created. Actually, wholeness is primarily a result of people's lifestyle. In turn, lifestyle has to do with the choices people make every day about what to eat, how to pray, and whether to save energy.

Choices tend to become habits. So wholeness is mainly dependent on people's habits. Habits are changeable with time. Wholeness depends on people recognizing the need to exchange their present habits for ones that lead to positive living and enhanced well-being for all of God's creation.

2. Assessing Wholeness

This exercise should help group members assess their present health practices (behaviors that maintain or improve health). Group members will likely disagree with some statements in the assessment. The statements reflect scientific knowledge, but in many areas current information is incomplete or answers are not simple. Healthy debate is a desired outcome of this exercise.

Directions

Members should complete the assessment individually. Try to be as honest as possible in evaluating your practices, recognizing that each of us has a long way to go to achieve wholeness. You are to circle each item in section A through M that is true for you. A scoring device for individuals and the group appears at the end of the assessment. After completion of the assessment and scoring, the leader should assist the members in sharing their findings.

Some items have notes that appear at the end of the book. You should read these notes.

Acknowledgments

The following wellness assessments were helpful in the preparation of this one.

Baldi, Susan, and others, *For Your Health: A Model for Self-Care* (South Laguna, Calif.: Nurses Model Health, 1980).

Pender, Nola J., *Health Promotion in Nursing Practice* (East Norwalk, Conn.: Appleton-Century-Crofts, 1982).

Ryan, Regina Sara, and John W. Travis, *Wellness Index* (Berkeley, Calif.: Ten Speed Press, 1981).

"Test Your MennoHealthStyle," *Sharing*, Mennonite Mutual Aid, Summer 1977.

Travis, John W., *Wellness Inventory* (Mill Valley, Calif.: Wellness Resource Center, 1977).

UWSP Institute for Lifestyle Improvement, *Lifestyle Assessment Questionnaire*, 2nd ed. (Stevens Point, Wis.: UWSP Foundation Press, 1980).

Assessment

A. Purpose

1. In the past year I have written down my life goals and considered how well I am accomplishing them.
2. My purposes in life reflect a good balance between concerns for God, other people, myself, and nature.
3. The kind of work I do reflects my values.
4. The way I use my time reflects what is most important to me and demonstrates caring.
5. I maintain a good balance between work and home relationships and activities.
6. The way I spend my money reflects nonconformity and concern for peace and justice.
7. I seek God's approval rather than the praise of people regarding my accomplishments.
8. My thoughts, feelings, and behaviors reflect a good balance between living in the past, the present, and the future.
9. My philosophy of life is more communal than individualistic.

B. Food

1. I read the labels of the foods I buy to check the ingredients.
2. I eat at least one raw fruit or vegetable daily.
3. I eat a dark green leafy or bright orange vegetable at least every other day.
4. I eat more poultry and fish than beef, pork, and lamb.
5. I omit meat at least two days a week and substitute non-meat complementary proteins.

6. I limit use of cured meats that contain nitrites (for example, bacon, hot dogs, ham, sausage, bologna).[1]
7. I seldom prepare or eat charcoal-broiled meat.[2]
8. I consciously decrease the amount of fat, especially saturated fat, in my diet.
9. In choosing margarine, I use one with a liquid food oil (not nonfood oils, for example, cottonseed oil) listed as the first ingredient.[3]
10. I avoid white bread and eat whole grain bread instead.
11. I do not add salt to my food at the table.
12. I seldom eat salty snack foods.
13. I do not add sugar to my food at the table.
14. I do not eat prepackaged cereals in which sugar is listed as the first ingredient.
15. I have sweet desserts three times a week or less.
16. I rarely suck hard candy, eat sticky candy, or chew gum with sugar in it.[4]
17. I deliberately control the amount of highly processed foods I eat.
18. I avoid processed foods containing coconut oil.[5]
19. I avoid buying food in cans with side seams.[6]
20. I divide my daily food intake into at least three regularly scheduled meals and seldom snack at unscheduled times.
21. I eat at fast-food restaurants once a week or less.
22. My meals are leisurely and relaxed.
23. My diet contains a variety of foods.
24. I maintain an appropriate weight.

C. Fluids
1. I take in six to eight cups of fluid daily.
2. I drink a citrus fruit juice (or eat the fruit instead) daily.
3. I do not drink sweetened, artificial fruit drinks.
4. I do not drink coffee, tea, or sodas that contain caffeine.[7]
5. I drink no more than two soft drinks a week.

6. I do not drink alcoholic beverages.
7. I do not drink extremely hot liquids.[8]
8. The water I drink is fluoridated.

D. Exercise

1. Some of my typical daily activities involve moderate or heavy physical exertion.
2. I do vigorous aerobic exercise (for example, brisk walking, jogging, swimming, bicycling, or rope jumping) for at least thirty minutes (or its equivalent, depending on the intensity of exercise) at least three days a week.
3. I do stretching-limbering exercises three or four days a week or more.
4. I avoid elevators and climb stairs instead.
5. I regularly walk or bicycle instead of driving to work, school, church, or the store.
6. I purposely park far enough away from my destination that I have to walk some to get there.
7. I do not sit for long periods with my legs crossed at the knees or wear constricting garments on my legs.[9]

E. Sleep

1. I usually sleep no more and no less than I need to in a day.
2. When I go to bed, I fall asleep easily.
3. If awakened at night, I can usually fall asleep easily again.
4. I sleep late occasionally, without feeling guilty.
5. I sleep on a firm surface.

F. Relaxation

1. I seldom rush around.
2. I do not interrupt people when they are talking or finish their sentences for them.
3. I have several hobbies I use to relax regularly.
4. I read at least six books a year just for relaxation.

5. I am at home during off-work hours at least four days a week.
6. I limit television watching to two hours or less a day.
7. I take at least two weeks of vacation each year.
8. I notice when I am tense and consciously relax myself.
9. I am aware of my particular signals of chronic stress and consciously respond to them by changing habits.
10. I do not bite my fingernails.
11. Each day I totally empty my mind and remain in a relaxed state for a period of time.
12. I often have periods of time when I have no structured or planned activities.
13. I regularly find a place to be alone, without feeling lonely.
14. I can easily leave what I am doing to meet other people's needs or to play with them.

G. Emotions

1. I enjoy my work.
2. I make time for things I enjoy.
3. I often say things to express joy.
4. I often laugh and enjoy it.
5. I sometimes laugh at myself.
6. I often look at my face and body with appreciation.
7. I concentrate without difficulty.
8. I make decisions after careful thought but without excessive wavering.
9. I trust my judgments.
10. I avoid negative thinking.
11. I have a planned time when I give myself positive affirmations (for example, "I am a good person") daily.
12. I do not chastise myself for making mistakes.
13. I do not hold onto bothersome thoughts or worries.
14. I use thoughts and behaviors to change my feelings.[10]
15. I cry sometimes.

16. I allow myself to grieve after a loss.
17. I set specific goals to help me accomplish things I want to do.
18. I do not procrastinate.
19. I frequently try new activities.
20. I seek help from professional counselors when needed.

H. Relationships

1. I frequently express love verbally to people close to me.
2. I often give compliments and affirmations to a number of people.
3. I accept compliments graciously.
4. I enjoy touching other people appropriately and do so.
5. I enjoy when other people touch me (in caring and appropriate ways).
6. I tend to trust other people.
7. I have a few close friends with whom I share mutually on a deep level frequently.
8. I have several people I can call on when I need aid (for example, for transportation or money).
9. I have one or more persons with whom I frequently discuss ideas.
10. I occasionally, but not constantly, spend time socializing with friends.
11. I frequently say I am sorry or admit that I was wrong to another person.
12. I sometimes talk in front of a group.
13. I sometimes communicate my weaknesses in a group.
14. I listen to others well and empathize with them easily.
15. I remember people's names.
16. I tolerate silence in a conversation.
17. I actively participate in group social events.
18. I initiate conversations with strangers easily.
19. I speak loudly enough that others can hear me easily.
20. I assert myself to ask for what I want from others.

21. I sometimes say no to people's requests without feeling guilty.
22. I express myself directly so people know where they stand with me.
23. I share my expectations of people with them and listen to their expectations of me.[11]
24. I am really me most of the time when I am with other people.
25. I usually react to criticism without being defensive.
26. I avoid blaming and criticizing others and use "I" messages in confronting other people.
27. I forgive others easily.
28. I express anger and frustration without hurting other people .
29. I express my physical sexual urges in ways that are wholesome and do not hurt me or other people.
30. I occasionally work with other people in carrying out a task overtime.
31. I relate to others as persons with equal rights regardless of sex, race, ethnicity, religion, age, marital status, economic status, or other differences.
32. I regularly relate to several people who are different from me in color or culture.
33. I often interact with my neighbors who live near me.

I. Spirituality

1. I regularly read the Bible, pray, and listen to what God is saying.
2. I am actively involved in a church and use my gifts for its ministries.
3. I regularly practice meaningful worship, silence, verbal sharing, confession, and celebration with a small group of believers.
4. I participate in group decision making in the church without insisting on my own way.

5. I actively participate in church activities at the international level.
6. I seek God's will and the counsel of the church in making important decisions.
7. I give at least one tenth of my income to meet the needs of persons who have less than I do.
8. I give some of my time without pay to people outside my family and friends when they are in need.
9. I often share my spiritual values with others.
10. I usually behave according to my moral principles.

J. Hygiene

1. When I am at home, I usually brush my teeth after every time I eat.
2. I use a soft toothbrush.
3. I use fluoridated toothpaste.
4. I floss my teeth daily.
5. I do not use permanent hair dyes.[12]

K. Checkups and Immunizations

1. Female: I check my breasts for lumps monthly and have a gynecological examination that includes a breast exam and Pap smear at least every three years.[13]
   Male: I check my testes for lumps regularly.
2. I regularly examine my lymph nodes for enlargement.[14]
3. I have determined an appropriate schedule for physical examinations and follow it.
4. I have determined an appropriate schedule for eye examinations and follow it.
5. I have my blood pressure checked at least every two years.
6. I have my cholesterol level checked at least every five years.
7. I have a dental checkup at least every one-two years.
8. I have a tetanus toxoid injection every ten years.

9. I have a diphtheria immunization every ten years.
10. I maintain a record of my immunizations.

L. Environmental Safety
1. I always wear a seat belt when I ride in a car.
2. I almost always drive within the speed limit.
3. I drive or ride less than 10,000 miles a year in a car.
4. The car I ride in most has radial tires.
5. The car I ride in most has disk brakes.
6. The car I ride in most has front seat head restraints that are adjusted high enough to protect against whiplash injuries.
7. When the traffic light turns yellow, I stop rather than hurrying through the intersection.
8. I stay at least one car length behind the car ahead of me for every ten miles per hour of speed.
9. The car I ride in most contains emergency flares or reflectors and a fire extinguisher.
10. The car I ride in most is serviced regularly.
11. I never drive after drinking alcohol or taking drugs that influence reaction time; nor do I ever ride with another driver under those conditions.
12. I do not smoke or chew tobacco.
13. No one smokes in my house or in my immediate work area.[15]
14. I rarely take nonprescription drugs.
15. I do not use drugs to relax, alter mood, or control weight or fatigue.
16. I keep medicines, cosmetics, cleaning fluids, and other chemicals where children cannot reach them.
17. The air where I live and work has a low pollution index.
18. I avoid extreme noise.
19. I am seldom exposed to sprays, chemical fumes, or exhaust gases.
20. I do not have a deep skin tan.[16]

21. There is a dry chemical fire extinguisher in the kitchen of the house where I live.
22. There is one or more smoke detectors mounted in the house where I live.
23. All floors, bathtubs, and showers in the house I live in are furnished to prevent falls from slippery or uneven surfaces.
24. The humidity in the house where I live is at least 60 percent year-round.
25. I consciously decrease my exposure to radiation.[17]

M. Global Awareness

1. I read at least one newspaper daily or one newsmagazine a week.
2. The house I live in is heated mostly by solar energy or wood.
3. The house I live in is well insulated.
4. The thermostat in the house I live in is kept at 68 degrees Fahrenheit or lower in cold weather.
5. I do not use an air conditioner regularly during hot weather. When I do use one, I keep the thermostat at 76 degrees Fahrenheit or higher.
6. The car I ride in most gets at least thirty miles per gallon with local driving.
7. I often car-pool or use public transportation for distance driving.
8. I consciously avoid overuse of energy in appliances, especially high-energy-consuming ones (for example, water heater, frost-free refrigerator, stove, clothes dryer, and dishwasher).
9. I avoid use of high-energy-consuming vehicles and electronic devices for recreation.
10. I daily consciously decrease my use of water, especially hot water.
11. I mostly use fluorescent lighting and turn off incandescent light when not in use.[18]

12. I avoid disposable products and keep to a minimum one-time use of household items made of nonbiodegradable or scarce materials (for example, plastics, Styrofoam, and aluminum foil).[19]

13. I regularly recycle paper, aluminum cans, and glass, and avoid using aerosol cans.[20]

14. The architecture, furnishings, and surrounding landscape of the house I live in were chosen to decrease upkeep (for example, repairs and lawn mowing), decrease heating and cooling requirements (for example, by shade trees), and reflect an inexpensive, conserving lifestyle.

15. I buy little unnecessary clothing.

16. I seldom use restaurants for entertainment or business.

17. My food buying often includes locally produced items.

18. I buy food in bulk at a food cooperative or similar store.

19. I grow some of my own food.

20. I return garbage, degradable household wastes, and leaves to the soil through composting and mulching.

21. I consciously avoid polluting the environment by minimizing use of pesticides, herbicides, phosphate-containing detergents, and leaded gasoline.

22. I am actively involved in at least one organization or activity for helping poor or oppressed people or for preserving life and nature.

23. I buy from a self-help organization.

24. I refuse to invest my money in organizations that oppress or destroy life and nature.

25. I live in a community of persons who share resources and provide support and accountability for a simple lifestyle.

Individual Scoring

To score yourself for each section of the assessment:

1. Add the number of items circled.

2. Multiply this number by the number of points per item (see number after the title of the section below).

3. Record your score on the appropriate line below.

4. Use a pencil or pen to color in the appropriate amount on the bar graph.

Your score suggests your degree of wholeness in terms of your health behavior in each area. The idea is not to compare yourself to others or to categorize yourself as poor, good, or excellent. Rather, the aim is to reach as high a level as possible.

Group Average

After each member has completed scoring, the leader should assist the group in obtaining group averages as a means of discovering where the majority are strongest and weakest. To figure the group average for a category of the assessment—

1. Add all the scores for that category.

2. Divide the sum by the number of people in the group.

Enter the group averages for each item next to your individual score. The group averages can be useful if the group chooses to change in the same area of behavior.

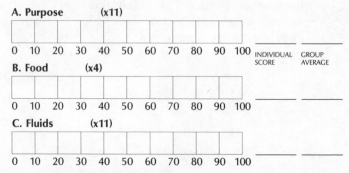

A. Purpose   (x11)

0   10   20   30   40   50   60   70   80   90   100   INDIVIDUAL   GROUP
SCORE   AVERAGE

B. Food   (x4)

0   10   20   30   40   50   60   70   80   90   100

C. Fluids   (x11)

0   10   20   30   40   50   60   70   80   90   100

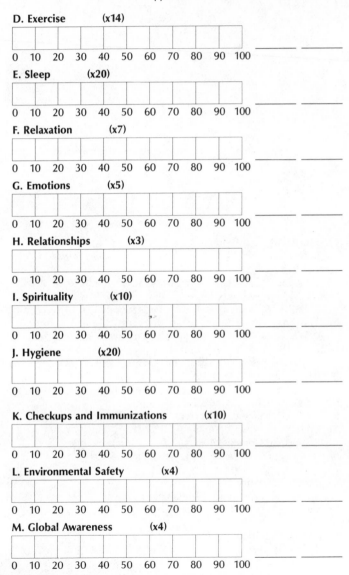

D. Exercise   (x14)

0   10   20   30   40   50   60   70   80   90   100

E. Sleep   (x20)

0   10   20   30   40   50   60   70   80   90   100

F. Relaxation   (x7)

0   10   20   30   40   50   60   70   80   90   100

G. Emotions   (x5)

0   10   20   30   40   50   60   70   80   90   100

H. Relationships   (x3)

0   10   20   30   40   50   60   70   80   90   100

I. Spirituality   (x10)

0   10   20   30   40   50   60   70   80   90   100

J. Hygiene   (x20)

0   10   20   30   40   50   60   70   80   90   100

K. Checkups and Immunizations   (x10)

0   10   20   30   40   50   60   70   80   90   100

L. Environmental Safety   (x4)

0   10   20   30   40   50   60   70   80   90   100

M. Global Awareness   (x4)

0   10   20   30   40   50   60   70   80   90   100

Notes

Chapter 1: A Life of Wholeness

1. Bruce Yoder, "The Gift of Healing," *Gospel Herald*, 5 Aug. 1980, p. 615.

2. Norman Cousins, "The Holistic Health Explosion," *Saturday Review*, 31 Mar. 1979, pp. 17-20.

3. *TAP #19 Health Care: Three Reports from 2030 A.D.* (Washington, D.C.: American Council of Life Insurance, 1980).

4. Walter Eichrodt, *Theology of the Old Testament*, vol 2., trans. J. A. Baker (Philadelphia: Westminster Press, 1967), p. 265.

5. Markus Barth, *Ephesians*, The Anchor Bible 34 (Garden City, N.Y.: Doubleday, 1974), p. 199.

Chapter 2: The Body, God's Temple

1. Carl E. Braaten and Lavonne Braaten, *The Living Temple* (New York: Harper & Row, 1976), pp. 11-12.

2. Norman Cousins, *Anatomy of an Illness as Perceived by the Patient* (New York: Bantam Books, 1981), pp. 136-154.

Chapter 3: Sexuality

1. Willard S. Krabill, "Human Sexuality for Christians," The Mennonite, 24 July 1979, p. 468.

Chapter 4: Nutrition

1. The Center for Science in the Public Interest (Suite 300, 1875

Connecticut Ave., N.W., Washington, DC 20009-5728) is a good source for information on nutrition questions including additives.

2. Doris Janzen Longacre, *More-with-Less Cookbook* (Scottdale, Pa.: Herald Press, 1976), p. 8.

3. Doris Janzen Longacre, *Living More with Less* (Scottdale, Pa.: Herald Press, 1980), pp. 16, 21.

4. Joan D. Gussow, *The Feeding Web: Issues in Nutritional Ecology* (Palo Alto, Calif.: Bull Publishing, 1978), p. 200.

5. Ronald J. Sider, *Rich Christians in an Age of Hunger: A Biblical Study* (Downers Grove, Ill.: InterVarsity Press, 1977), p. 48.

6. Richard J. Foster, *Freedom of Simplicity* (San Francisco: Harper & Row, 1981), p. 115.

7. *Children's Prayers from Around the World* (New York: William H. Sadlier, 1981), p. 26.

Chapter 5: Physical Fitness

1. John W. Farquhar, *The American Way of Life Need Not Be Hazardous to Your Health* (New York: W. W. Norton, 1978), p. 82.

Chapter 6: Mental Health

1. Henri J. M. Nouwen, *Reaching Out: The Three Movements of the Spiritual Life* (Garden City, N.Y.: Doubleday, 1975).

Chapter 7: Stress

1. During a serious illness Norman Cousins decided to test the proposition that the opposite case is true—positive emotions produce positive chemical changes in the body. Feeling that one of the causes of his illness was exhaustion, he embarked on a systematic program of watching amusing movies and reading humor books. In *Anatomy of an Illness as Perceived by the Patient* (ch. 1) he attributes his recovery partly to the good medicine of laughter.

2. Robert McAfee Brown, *Creative Dislocation: The Movement of Grace, Journeys in Faith*, ed. Robert A. Raines (Nashville: Abingdon Press, 1980), p. 134.

Chapter 8: Deterrents to Wholeness

1. W. R. Spence, M.D., *The Medical Consequences of Alcoholism* (Waco, Tex.: Health Edco, Inc. 1987).

2. John Bertsche, "The Church's Attitude Toward Alcohol," Normal, Ill., Mennonite Church of Normal, 1985 (photocopy).

3. Willard S. Krabill, " 'Miller-Time'? For Mennonites?" (photocopy).

4. Long, Robert Emmet, *Drugs and American Society* (New York: H. W. Wilson Co., 1986), p. 59.

5. Child Study Association of America, *You, Your Child and Drugs* (New York: Child Study Press, 1971), pp. 67-68.

Chapter 9: The Global Environment

1. Loren Wilkinson, *Earthkeeping: Christian Stewardship of Natural Resources* (Grand Rapids: William B. Eerdmans Co., 1980), p. 226.

2. Harold K. Schilling, "The Whole Earth Is the Lord's," in Ian G. Barbour, ed., *Earth Might Be Fair* (Englewood Cliffs, N.J.: Prentice-Hall, 1972), pp. 109-110.

3. Denis Hayes, *Repairs, Reuse, Recycling: First Steps to a Sustainable Society*, Worldwatch Paper 23 (Washington, D.C.: Worldwatch Institute, 1978), p. 5.

4. Doris Janzen Longacre, *Living More with Less* (Scottdale, Pa.: Herald Press, 1980), p. 47.

5. Richard J. Foster, *Freedom of Simplicity* (San Francisco: Harper & Row, 1981), p. 164.

6. Longacre, p. 48.

Chapter 10: Toward Spiritual Wholeness

1. Richard J. Foster, *Celebration of Discipline: The Path to Spiritual Growth* (San Francisco: Harper & Row, 1978), p. 6.

2. Henri J. M. Nouwen, *Reaching Out: The Three Movements of the Spiritual Life* (Garden City, N.Y.: Doubleday, 1975), p. 87.

3. Nouwen, p. 89.

4. Nouwen, p. 80.

Chapter 11: Responsibility for Wholeness

1. Margery Williams, *The Velveteen Rabbit* (New York: Avon Books, 1975), p. 17.

2. Richard J. Foster, *Celebration of Discipline: The Path to Spiritual Growth* (San Francisco: Harper & Row, 1978), pp. 8-9.

3. Ibid., p. 69.

4. Ibid., p. 75.

5. Ibid., pp. 78-83.

6. Ibid., pp. 163-164.

7. Ibid., p. 167.

Chapter 12: Wholeness Through the Church

1. Harold S. Bender, *These Are My People*, Conrad Grebel Lectures, 1960 (Scottdale, Pa.: Herald Press, 1962); see chs. 1–3.

2. Richard J. Foster, *Celebration of Discipline: The Path to Spiritual Growth* (San Francisco: Harper & Row, 1978), p. 138.

3. Dietrich Bonhoeffer, *Life Together* (New York: Harper & Row, 1954), p. 97.

4. Ray C. Stedman, *Body Life* (Glendale, Calif.: Regal Books, 1972), pp. 39-40.

5. Paul M. Miller, *Leading the Family of God* (Scottdale, Pa.: Herald Press, 1981), p. 37.

6. Foster, p. 127.

7. Howard A. Snyder, *The Community of the King* (Downers Grove, Ill.: InterVarsity Press, 1977), p. 71.

8. Bender, p. 44.

9. Bender, p. 44.

10. Snyder, p. 64.

11. Foster, pp. 163-171.

Appendix: Adventures in Wholeness

1. Nitrites have been implicated as possible cancer-producing agents. See "Nitrites and Nitrosamines: Is the Hot Dog an Endangered Species?" *Consumer Reports*, May 1980, pp. 310-311; "Nitrosamines: Reason Enough to Give Up Bacon?" *Consumer Reports*, September 1981, p. 499.

2. Charcoal-broiled meat and its smoke may be carcinogenic (cancer-producing). See W. Lijinsky and P. Shubik, "Benzo (a) pyrene and Other Polynuclear Hydrocarbons in Charcoal-Broiled Meat," *Science*, July 3, 1964, pp. 53-55; "Commoner Attack on Big Mac, et al," *Science News*, 20 May 1978, pp. 326-327.

3. Liquid food oils contain less saturated fat than partially hydrogenated ones. In addition, nonfood crops (for example, cotton) may receive extra chemical sprays. See Nikki Goldbeck and David Goldbeck, *The Supermarket Handbook; Access to Whole Foods*, rev. ed. (New York: The American Library, 1976), pp. 43-44.

4. Dental caries are most apt to follow prolonged and frequent exposure to sugar. Sticky candy, hard candy, and chewing gum all increase exposure time. See James H. Shaw, "Dietary Considerations in Oral Health," *Family and Community Health; The Journal of Health Promotion and Maintenance 3* (3):51-60 (1980).

5. Coconut oil is high in saturated fat and is part of many processed foods, for example, nondairy creamers.

6. Side seams are fastened by solder, which contains lead. See Dorothy M. Settle and Clair C. Patterson, "Lead in Albacore: Guide to Lead Pollution in Americans," *Science*, 14 March 1980, pp. 1167-1176.

7. Sodas containing caffeine include colas, Mr. Pibb, Mountain Dew, Mello Yello, Tab, Sunkist Orange, and Dr. Pepper. Caffeine-free sodas are 7-Up, Sprite, Fresca, Hines Root Beer, Patio Orange, and Fanta Orange. See "Caffeine: How to Consume Less," *Consumer Reports*, October 1981, pp. 597-599.

8. Some evidence exists that temperature extremes cause cracking of tooth enamel. See Elaine D. Dyer, Mary A. Monson, and Maxine J. Cope, "Dental Health in Adults," *American Journal of Nursing* 76:1156-59 (1976).

9. Crossing your legs at the knees or wearing constricting leg garments retards venous circulation and possibly can contribute to problems of the venous system.

10. Psychologists suggest that our thoughts often result in our feeling badly and that, therefore, changing thoughts can change feelings. Likewise, attitude change can follow efforts to behave differently. For one popular book on this topic, see Wayne W. Dyer, *Your Erroneous Zones* (New York: Avon Books, 1976). Note that Dyer takes an individualistic approach, rather than the community focus of this book.

11. Conflict is often a result of unshared, conflicting expectations on the part of persons involved.

12. Chemicals in hair dyes, especially permanent ones, have been implicated as possibly causing cancer. See "Are Hair Dyes Safe?" *Consumer Reports*, August 1979, pp. 456-460; Frances Weinberg, "Highlights on Hair Dyes," *Consumers' Research Magazine*, September 1980, pp. 19-21.

13. Current recommendations for Pap smears have been liberalized to suggest that every three years is adequate for mass screening after two initial negative tests a year apart. However, individuals may choose more frequent testing.

Women over forty should have a pelvic and breast examination yearly. For a detailed report see "ACS Report on the Cancer-Related Health Checkup," *Ca: A Cancer Journal for Clinicians 30* (4): 194-240 (1980). A summary of the recommendations is available in David M. Eddy, "Early Detection," *World Health*, September-October 1981, pp. 18-20.

14. Lymph node examination, while not commonly done by lay people and requiring learning from health professionals, could decrease cancer deaths through early detection.

15. Experts now rank it (other people's smoke) as the third leading cause of preventable deaths in this country, exceeded only by active smoking and alcohol. *University of California at Berkeley Wellness Letter*, Oct. 1991.

16. Skin cancer is more frequent in persons with heavy exposure to the sun.

17. Excessive radiation is linked to cancer, although little is known about effects of low dosages. Frequent X rays, occupational exposure, and high natural background radiation (for example, in Colorado) may increase risk.

18. Fluorescent lights require less energy than incandescent lights.

19. Nonbiodegradable products are materials that do not decompose and so become waste problems.

20. Aerosol cans are dangerous to dispose of and are not reusable.

Bibliography

Allen, David E., and others, eds. *Whole-Person Medicine*. Downers Grove, Ill.: InterVarsity Press, 1980.

Allen, Robert F., and Shirley Linde. *Lifegain: The Exciting New Program That Will Change Your Health—And Your Life*. New York: Appleton-Century-Crofts, 1981.

Ardell, Donald B. *High Level Wellness: An Alternative to Doctors, Drugs and Disease*. Emmaus, Pa.: Rodale Press, 1979.

Baily, Covert. *Fit or Fat?* Boston: Houghton Mifflin, 1978.

Barnhouse, Ruth Tiffany, and Urban T. Holmes, eds., *Male Female: Christian Approaches to Sexuality*. New York: Seabury Press, 1976.

Bender, Harold S. *These Are My People*. Conrad Grebel Lectures, 1960. Scottdale, Pa.: Herald Press, 1962.

Benson, Herbert, and Miriam Z. Klipper. *The Relaxation Response*. New York: William, Morrow, 1975.

Birch, Bruce C., and Larry L. Rasmussen. *The Predicament of the Prosperous*. Philadelphia: Westminster Press, 1978.

Bonhoeffer, Dietrich. *Life Together*. New York: Harper & Row, 1954.

Bottomley, Frank. *Attitudes to the Body in Western Christendom*. London: Lepus Books, 1979.

Braaten, Carl E. and LaVonne. *The Living Temple*. New York: Harper & Row, 1976.

Brand, Paul, and Philip Yancey. *Fearfully and Wonderfully Made*. Grand Rapids: Zondervan, 1980.

Brecher, Edward M., and the editors of *Consumer Reports*. *Licit and Illicit Drugs*. Boston: Little, Brown, 1972.

Brody, Jane. *Jane Brody's Nutrition Book: A Lifetime Guide to Good Eating for Better Health and Weight Control by the Personal Health Columnist of the New York Times*. New York: W. W. Norton, 1981.

Brown, Barbara B. *New Mind, New Body*. New York: Harper & Row, 1974.

Brown, Lester R. *Building a Sustainable Society*. New York: W. W. Norton, 1981.

_____. *The Twenty-Ninth Day*. New York: W. W. Norton, 1978.

Brueggemann, Walter. *Living Toward a Vision*. Philadelphia: United Church Press, 1976.

Caes, David, ed. *Caring for the Least of These*. Scottdale, Pa.: Herald Press, 1992.

Center for Science in the Public Interest. *Ninety-Nine Ways to a Simple Lifestyle*. Garden City, N.Y.: Doubleday, 1976.

Cesaretti, C. A., and Stephen Commins, eds. *Let the Earth Bless the Lord*. New York: Seabury Press, 1981.

Child Study Association of America. *You, Your Child and Drugs*. New York: Child Study Press, 1971.

Commoner, Barry. *The Closing Circle*. New York: Alfred A. Knopf, 1971.

Cooper, Kenneth H. *The New Aerobics*. New York: Bantam Books, 1970.

Cosby, Gordon. *Handbook for Mission Groups*. Waco, Tex. Word Books, 1975.

Cousins, Norman. *Anatomy of an Illness as Perceived by the Patient*. New York: Bantam Books, 1981.

Dodge, David W. *Social Stress and Chronic Illness*. Notre Dame, Ind.: Univ. of Notre Dame Press, 1970.

Farquhar, Hohn W. *The American Way of Life Need Not Be Hazardous to Your Health*. New York: W. W. Norton, 1978.

Fenton, John Y., ed. *Theology and Body*. Philadelphia: Westminster Press, 1974.

Foster, Richard J. *Celebration of Discipline: The Path to Spiritual Growth*. San Francisco: Harper & Row, 1978.

_____. Freedom of Simplicity. San Francisco: Harper & Row, 1981.

Fowler, Jim, and Sam Keen. *Life Maps: Conversations on the Journey of Faith*. Waco, Tex.: Word Books, 1978.

Gleason, John J., Jr. *Growing Up to God: Eight Steps in Religious Development*. Nashville: Abingdon, 1975.

Heller, Alfred L. *Your Body, His Temple*. Nashville: Thomas Nelson, 1981.

Heggen, Carolyn Holderread. *Sexual Abuse in Christian Homes and Churches*. Scottdale, Pa.: Herald Press, 1993.

Jeffrey, D. Balfour, and Roger C. Katz. *Take It Off and Keep It Off: A Behavioral Program for Weight Loss and Healthy Living*. Englewood Cliffs, N.J.: Prentice Hall, 1977.

Kelsey, Morton T. *Adventure Inward*. Minneapolis: Augsburg, 1980.

Kinney, Jean, and Gwen Leaton. *Loosening the Grip: A Handbook of Alcohol Information*. St. Louis: C. V. Mosby, 1978.

Kraus, C. Norman. *The Community of the Spirit*. Grand Rapids: William B. Eerdmans, 1974; 2d. ed., Scottdale, Pa.: Herald Press, 1993.

Kreider, Alan. *Journey Towards Holiness: A Way of Living for God's Nation*. Scottdale, Pa.: Herald Press, 1987.

Lappe, France Moore. *Diet for a Small Planet*, rev. ed. New York: Ballantine Books, 1975.

Larson, Bruce. *There's a Lot More to Health Than Not Being Sick*. Waco, Tex.: Word Books, 1981.

Lawrence, Brother. *The Practice of the Presence of God*. Old Tappan, N.J.: Fleming H. Revell, 1958.

Leech, Kenneth. *Soul Friend*. San Francisco: Harper & Row, 1977.

Lehman, Donna. *What on Earth Can You Do?* Scottdale, Pa.: Herald Press, 1993.

Longacre, Doris Janzen. *Living More with Less*. Scottdale: Pa.: Herald Press, 1980.

_____. *More-with-Less Cookbook*. Scottdale, Pa.: Herald Press, 1976.

McGinnis, James and Kathleen. *Parenting for Peace and Justice*. Maryknoll, N.Y.: Orbis Books, 1981.

McKeown, Thomas. *The Role of Medicine*. Princeton, N.J.: Princeton Univ. Press, 1980.

Mahoney, Michael J. and Kathryn. *Permanent Weight Control: A Total Solution to the Dieter's Dilemma*. New York: W. W. Norton, 1976.

Meyer, Art and Jocele. *Earthkeepers: Environmental Perspectives on Hunger, Poverty, and Injustice.* Scottdale, Pa.: Herald Press, 1991.

Miller, John W. *A Christian Approach to Sexuality*. Scottdale, Pa.: Mennonite Publishing House, 1973.

Moltmann, Jurgen. *The Church in the Power of the Spirit: A Contribution to Messianic Ecclesiology*. Trans. Margaret Kohl. New York: Harper & Row, 1977.

_____. *The Future of Creation*: Collected Essays. Trans. Margaret Kohl. Philadelphia: Fortress Press, 1979.

Morehouse, Laurence E. *Total Fitness in Thirty Minutes a Week*. New York: Simon and Schuster, 1975.

Nelson, Jack. *Hunger for Justice*. Maryknoll, N.Y.: Orbis Books, 1980.

Nelson, John B. *Embodiment: An Approach to Sexuality and Christian Theology*. Minneapolis: Augsburg, 1978.

Nouwen, Henri J. M. *Reaching Out: The Three Movements of the Spiritual Life*. Garden City, N.Y.: Doubleday, 1975.

Oates, Wayne E. *Religious Factors in Mental Illness*. New York: Association Press, 1955.

O'Connor, Elizabeth. *Our Many Selves*. New York: Harper & Row, 1971.

Pilch, John J. Wellness: *Your Invitation to Full Life*. Minneapolis: Winston Press, 1981.

Pittenger, Norman. *Making Sexuality Human: Love and Control in Sexuality*. New York: Pilgrim Press, 1979.

Postman, Neil. *The Disappearance of Childhood*. New York: Delacorte Press, 1982.

Powers, Edward A. *Human Sexuality: A Preliminary Study*. New York: Pilgrim Press, 1977.

Raines, Robert A. *New Life in the Church*, rev. ed. New York: Harper & Row, 1980.

Rifkin, Jeremy. *Entropy: A New Yorld View*. New York: Viking Press, 1980.

Rogers, Carl R. *On Becoming a Person*. Boston: Houghton Mifflin, 1961.

Sale, Kirkpatrick. *Human Scale*. New York: Coward, McCann and Geoghegan, 1980.

Schlabach, Joetta Handrich, with Burnett, Kristina Mast. *Extending the Table: A World Community Cookbook*. Scottdale, Pa.: Herald Press, 1991.

Selye, Hans. *The Stress of Life*. New York: McGraw-Hill, 1976.

_____. *Stress Without Distress*. New York: New American Library, 1975.

Shutt, Joyce M. *Steps to Hope*. Scottdale, Pa.: Herald Press, 1990.

Sider, Ronald J., ed. *Cry Justice: The Bible on Hunger and Poverty*. Ramsey, N.J.: Paulist Press, 1980.

_____. *Rich Christians in an Age of Hunger: A Biblical Study*. Downers Grove, Ill.: InterVarsity Press, 1977.

Simple Living Collective. *Taking Charge: Achieving Personal and Political Change Through Simple Living*. San Francisco: American Friends Service Committee, 1977.

Snyder, Howard A. *The Problem of Wineskins*. Downers Grove, Ill.: InterVarsity Press, 1975.

Southard, Samuel. *Christians and Mental Health*. Nashville: Broadman Press, 1972.

Stedman, Ray C. *Body Life*. Glendale, Calif.: Regal Books, 1972.

Tanner, Ogden. *Stress*. New York: Time-Life Books, 1976.

Toton, Suzanne C. *World Hunger: The Responsibility of Christian Education*. Maryknoll, N.Y.: Orbis Books, 1982.

Vickery, Donald M., and James F. Fries. *Take Care of Yourself: A Consumer's Guide to Medical Care* 4th. ed. Reading, Mass.: Addison-Wesley, 1989.

Westberg, Granger E., ed. *Theological Roots of Wholistic Health Care*. Hinsdale, Ill.: Wholistic Health Centers, 1979.

Wilkinson, Loren, ed. *Earthkeeping: Christian Stewardship of Natural Resources*. Grand Rapids: William B. Erdmans, 1980.